CONTENTS

PAGES 4-5 Characters and Icons **PAGES 6-7** World Map

UNIT 1 — PAGES 8-17

- **VOCABULARY**
  hello, hi, goodbye, bye
  mom, dad, brother, sister, grandma, grandpa
- **GRAMMAR**
  What's your name?
  My name's …
  This is my …
- **FEATURES**
  Country: USA
  World Music Song: I Love My Family
  Phonics: a, o, h, t

UNIT 2 — PAGES 18-27

- **VOCABULARY**
  panda, tiger, fish, monkey, elephant, octopus
  desk, pencil case, board, door, window, clock
- **GRAMMAR**
  What is it?
  It's a / an …
  Is it a / an … ?
  Yes, it is. / No, it isn't.
- **FEATURES**
  Country: China
  World Music Song: Follow Me!
  Phonics: u, c, m, d

PAGES 28-29 Progress Check Units 1 & 2 **PAGES 30-31** Steam Challenge 1

UNIT 3 — PAGES 32-41

- **VOCABULARY**
  one, two, three, four, five, six, seven, eight, nine, ten
  pen, pencil, eraser, book, ruler, backpack
- **GRAMMAR**
  How old are you?
  I'm …
  one book / two books
  one pen / three pens
- **FEATURES**
  Country: Russia
  World Music Song: Counting Song
  Phonics: e, i, p, b

UNIT 4 — PAGES 42-51

- **VOCABULARY**
  teacher, actor, doctor, farmer, cook, artist
  singer, dancer, taekwondo instructor, engineer, inventor, soccer player
- **GRAMMAR**
  His / Her name's …
  He's / She's a / an …
  He / She isn't a / an …
  Is he / she a / an … ?
  Yes, he / she is. /
  No, he / she isn't.
- **FEATURES**
  Country: Spain
  World Music Song: Working People
  Phonics: s, y, f, x

PAGES 52-53 Progress Check Units 3 & 4 **PAGES 54-55** Steam Challenge 2

UNIT 5 — PAGES 56-65

- **VOCABULARY**
  doll, computer game, teddy bear, robot, bike, kite
  red, yellow, blue, green, pink, brown, gray, white, black, orange
- **GRAMMAR**
  What are they?
  They're …
  Are they (color)?
  Yes, they are. /
  No, they aren't.
- **FEATURES**
  Country: Egypt
  World Music Song: Teddy Bears For You!
  Phonics: w, k, g, q, r

UNIT 6 — PAGES 66-75

VOCABULARY
cat, dog, rabbit, turtle, bird, horse

snake, spider, iguana, mouse, frog, hamster

GRAMMAR
I have a / an …
I don't have a / an …

Do you have a / an … ?
Yes, I do. / No, I don't.

FEATURES
Country: Mexico
World Music Song: Do You Have a Pet?
Phonics: l, j, z, v, n

PAGES 76-77 **Progress Check Units 5 & 6**   PAGES 78-79 **Steam Challenge 3**

UNIT 7 — PAGES 80-89

VOCABULARY
hair, eyes, ears, nose, mouth, teeth

legs, arms, feet, hands, fingers, toes

GRAMMAR
He / She / It has …

Does he / she / it have … ?
Yes, he / she / it does. /
No, he / she / it doesn't.

FEATURES
Country: India
World Music Song: Happy Body Song
Phonics: ll, zz

UNIT 8 — PAGES 90-99

VOCABULARY
pool, park, mall, stadium, school, zoo

tree, river, beach, mountain, flower, lake

GRAMMAR
There's a / an …
There isn't a / an …

Is there a … ?
Yes, there is. /
No, there isn't.

FEATURES
Country: UK
World Music Song: Way Up High
Phonics: ss, ff

PAGES 100-101 **Progress Check Units 7 & 8**   PAGES 102-103 **Steam Challenge 4**

UNIT 9 — PAGES 104-113

VOCABULARY
apple, banana, pear, orange, pineapple, watermelon

eleven, twelve, thirteen, fourteen, fifteen, sixteen, seventeen, eighteen, nineteen, twenty

GRAMMAR
There's one …
There are (number) …s.

How many …s are there?
There are (number) …s.

FEATURES
Country: Brazil
World Music Song: Amazing Mrs. Fruity
Phonics: ch, sh

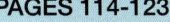

UNIT 10 — PAGES 114-123

VOCABULARY
table, closet, TV, bed, sofa, chair

bedroom, bathroom, living room, kitchen, garage, yard

GRAMMAR
The … is in / on / under the …

Where's the … ?
It's in / on / under the …
Where are the …s?
They're in / on / under the …

FEATURES
Country: Japan
Phonics: nk, ng

PAGES 124-125 **Progress Check Units 9 & 10**   PAGES 126-127 **Steam Challenge 5**

 PAGE 128 **GRAMMAR GUIDE**

CHARACTERS AND ICONS

Hi! I'm Eddie. Welcome to Next Station!

My name's Beakie. Let's learn English!

LOOK AND DO / LISTEN AND DO
Activities to interpret the picture of the unit opener pages

LISTEN
Audio tracks to practice listening skills

WORLD MUSIC
Songs with a World Music flavor

TEMPLATE
Photocopiable Language File activities to use in class

 **BE** sociable and creative. Know yourself!

 **THINK** critically when you use information!

 **LEARN** to do things by yourself. Learn how to learn!

 **COLLABORATE / COMMUNICATE** with others. Teamwork is cool!

 **ACT** respectfully, be tolerant, and friendly!

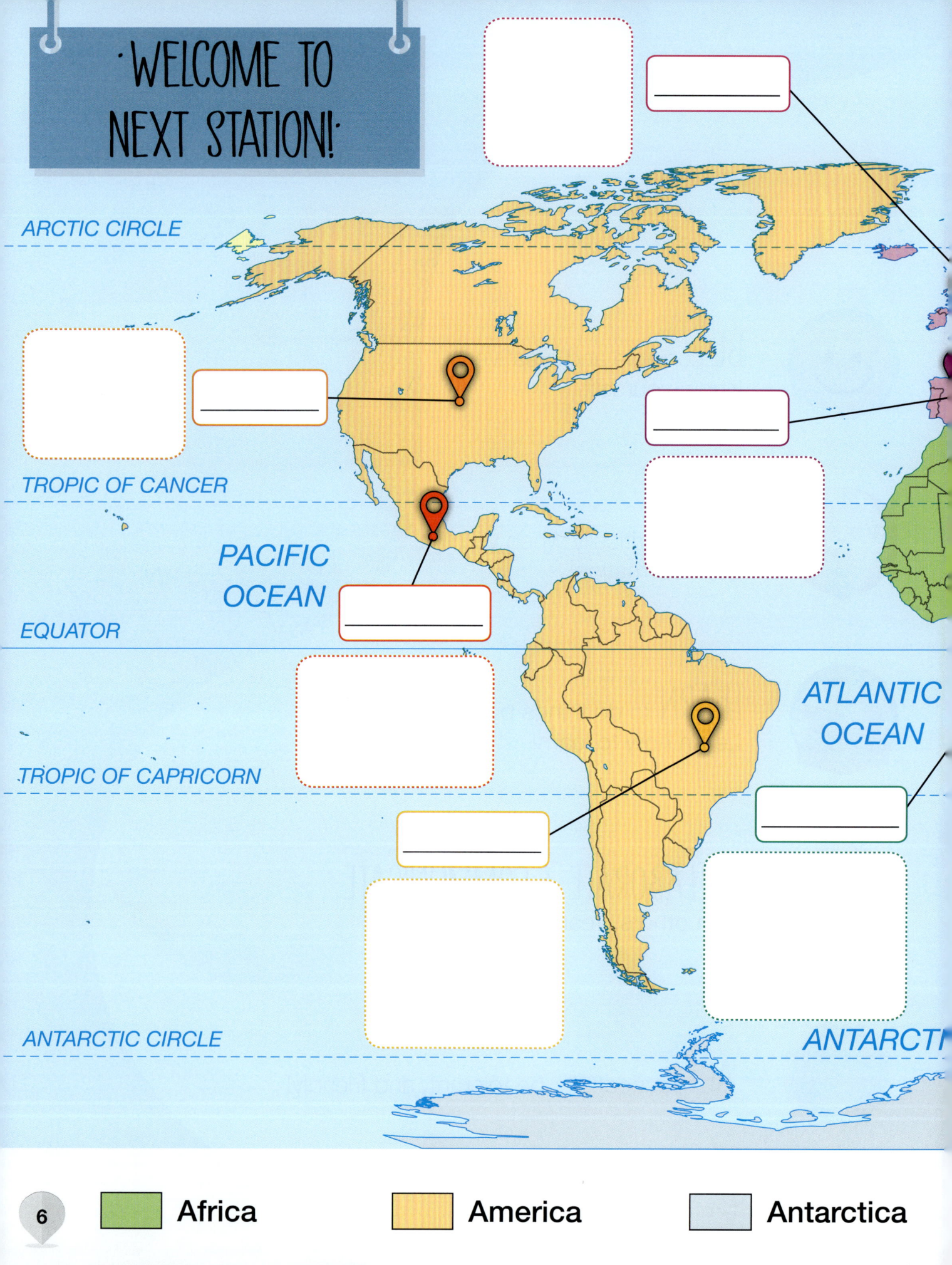

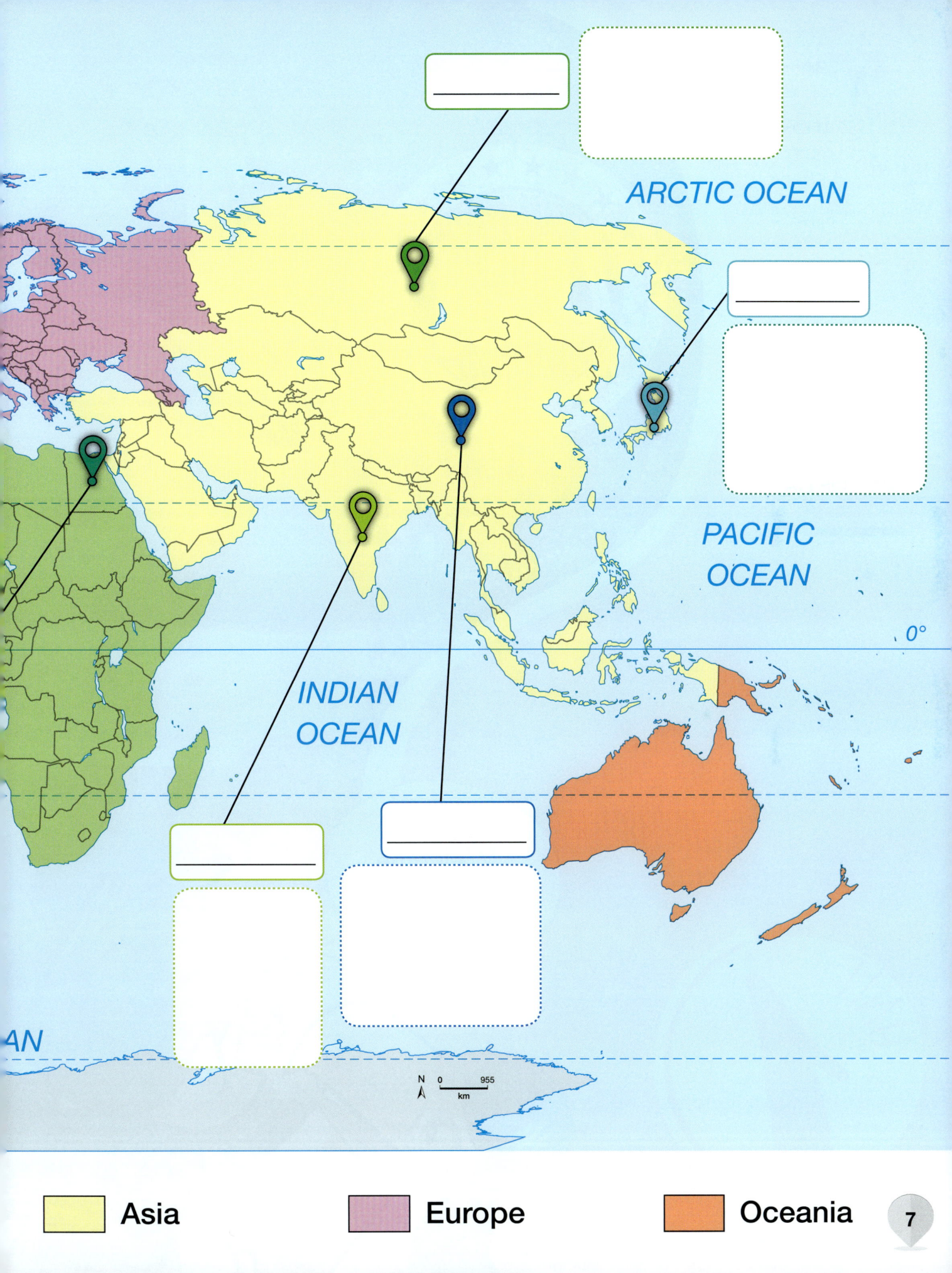

UNIT 1 Lesson 1

VOCABULARY

TRACK 3

1 Listen and read.

 **2** Make a line. Talk to a friend.

WORKBOOK page 4

Lesson 2

1 Listen and read.

> Hi, I'm Hannah. What's your name?
>
> My name's Beakie.
>
> Look! Eddie!
>
> Hi, Eddie.
>
> Bye, Hannah!
>
> Goodbye, Hannah!

GRAMMAR

What's your name?
My name's Hannah.
My name's Beakie.
(**My name's** Beakie. = **I'm** Beakie.)

2 Match to the correct answers.

What's your name?

I'm Hannah.

Bye, Eddie!

Hello, Hannah!

My name's Beakie.

Lesson 3

SOUNDS GREAT

 TRACK 5

1 Listen and chant.

Hi! I'm Oscar.

I'm a cat.

I'm hot.

Look at my hat.

 TRACK 6

2 Listen and say.

hat   hot

 TRACK 7

3 Look, listen, and connect.

1    h 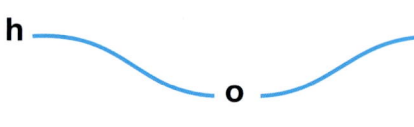 t
                              o

2    a

            h   t

 4 Read the chant and underline *a*, *o*, *h*, and *t*.

12

WORKBOOK page 6

Lesson 4 — READING TIME

 **1** Listen and read.

1
- Hi! I'm Ken. Welcome!
- Hi! I'm Oliver.

2
- What's your name?
- I'm Anna. I'm hot!
- Nice hat!

3
- What's your name?
- I'm Tim.

4
- Let's be friends!

 **2** Read the story again. Check (✓) the **value**.

Say hello. ○   Be friendly. ○

 3 Circle the friendly words.

Hi! / hot / Welcome! / hat

WORKBOOK page 7

Lesson 5

 1 Listen, point, and say.

1. brother
2. mom
3. dad
4. grandpa
5. sister
6. grandma

 2 Listen and circle.

1. sister / brother
2. mom / dad
3. grandma / grandpa
4. sister / brother

 3 Sing. **I Love My Family**.

Hello, Grandma.
I love you.
Hello, Jim.
I love you, too.

Hello, Grandpa.
I love you.
Hello, Jim.
I love you, too.

Hello, Mom.
I love you.
Hello, Jim.
I love you, too.

Hello, Dad.
I love you.
Hello, Jim.
I love you, too.

Lesson 6

GRAMMAR
This is my mom.

TRACK 12

1 Listen, read, and say.

2 Draw, write, and say.

WORKBOOK page 9

GRAMMAR GUIDE page 129

Lesson 7

FUN READER

LET'S VISIT THE USA

1 Read about a family in the USA.

Hi, I'm Greg. This is my brother, Al.

Hi! I'm a cowboy. The USA is famous for cowboys.

This is my sister, Helen.

Hello. Look! This is a hamburger. Mmm! Delicious! The USA is famous for hamburgers.

Think Twice

1 Read and circle.
The USA is famous for cowboys and hamburgers.
True / False

2 Can you name another thing the USA is famous for?

Lesson 8 · SPEAKING TIME ·

1 Draw, write, and say.

> The USA is famous for hamburgers. What's your country famous for?

> My country is famous for _____.

NEW FRIENDS

1 Complete the conversation. Choose your response.

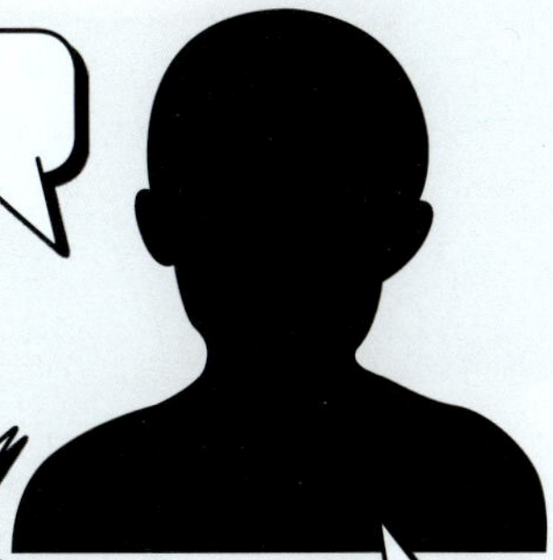

- Hello.
- I'm Al. What's your name?
- How are you?
- Hi!
- My name's _____.

I'm fine. ◯
I'm OK. ◯

2 Act out the conversation.

Lesson 1

·VOCABULARY·

TRACK 13

1 Listen, point, and say.

1 panda
2 tiger
3 fish
4 monkey
5 elephant
6 octopus

2 Look and check (✓) or cross (✗).

1 an octopus ◯
2 a tiger ◯
3 a monkey ◯
4 a fish ◯
5 an elephant ◯
6 a panda ◯

3 Draw, write, and say.

This is my animal sanctuary.

This is an octopus.

WORKBOOK page 11

Lesson 2

🔊 TRACK 14

1 Listen and read.

· GRAMMAR ·

What is it?
It's a panda.
It's an elephant.
(an + a, e, i, o, u)

 **2** Connect the words.

It's a ——— panda.

            octopus.

It's an   elephant.

            monkey.

 **3** Play the Animal Game.

WORKBOOK page 12

GRAMMAR GUIDE page 129

Unit 2 · Lesson 3 — SOUNDS GREAT

TRACK 15
1 Listen and chant.

Mom! Dad!
A cat is in the hut.

TRACK 16
2 Listen and say.

u   c   m   d

hut   cat   mom   dad

TRACK 17
3 Look, listen, and connect.

1   m — o — m

2   d   d
           a

3   c   t
           a

4   h   t
           u

4 Read the chant and underline *u*, *c*, *m*, and *d*.

WORKBOOK page 13

Lesson 4 ·REDING TIME·

1 Listen and read.

1 Bye, Mom. Bye, Dad.

2 Stop! Oops! Sorry, cat.

3 Hi, David! What's up? Stop! A car!

4 Please, be careful. Sorry.

 **2** Read the story again. Check (✓) the **value** ⭐.

Be careful. ◯   Say hi and bye. ◯

 **3** Read and circle.

I **look** / **sing** and **listen** / **walk** to be careful.

WORKBOOK page 14

Lesson 5 · VOCABULARY·

1 Listen, point, and say.

1. desk
2. pencil case
3. board
4. door
5. window
6. clock

 2 Point, ask, and answer.

What is it?

It's a desk.

 3 Sing and act. **Follow Me!**

Stand up, please.
And walk to the board.
Wave to your friends,
And walk to the door.

Now walk to the window,
Turn around.
Walk to your desk,
And please sit down.

WORKBOOK page 15

Lesson 6

GRAMMAR

Is it a clock?
Yes, **it is.** / No, **it isn't.**

TRACK 21

1 Listen, read, and say.

2 Look at Activity 1 and circle.

1 Is it a clock?   Yes, it is. / No, it isn't.
2 Is it a desk?   Yes, it is. / No, it isn't.

 **3** Play the Guessing Game.

WORKBOOK page 16   GRAMMAR GUIDE page 129

Lesson 7 · FUN READER ·

LET'S VISIT CHINA

1 Read about animals from China.

Hi! I'm Chen. Look! What is it?

Is it a lion?
Yes, it is. It isn't a real animal.
It's a traditional costume from China.

It's a panda.
Its name is Cong Cong.
It's in an animal sanctuary in China.

Think Twice

1 Read and circle the true sentence.
It's a real panda.
It's a real lion.

2 Which animal do you prefer?

Lesson 8 SPEAKING TIME

1 Draw and write.

_____ is a traditional festival in my country.

NEW FRIENDS

1 Complete the conversation. Choose your response.

Hello! I'm Chen. This is Dan.

Hi! I'm _____.
This is _____.

Nice to meet you.

Nice to meet you, too. ○

Hi! How are you? ○

2 Act out the conversation.

WORKBOOK
page 17

# PROGRESS CHECK

 1 Read and check (✓).

What's your name?

I'm Ben. ◯

My name's Anna. ◯

This is my …

brother. ◯

sister. ◯

 **2** Read and match.

1 My   your name?
2 This   name's Rob.
3 What's   is my sister.

THINK AGAIN!

A famous food in the USA is _____.

My favorite picture is on page _____.

A famous place in the USA is _____.

WORKBOOK page 18   STICKERS   PASSPORT page 2

PROGRESS CHECK

✅ **1** Read and circle *a* or *an*.

1 It's **(a)** / **an** window.
2 It's **a** / **an** elephant.
3 It's **a** / **an** clock.
4 It's **a** / **an** fish.
5 It's **a** / **an** octopus.
6 It's **a** / **an** tiger.

✅ **2** Look and circle.

❶ Is it a lion?
Yes, it is. / (No, it isn't.)

❷ Is it a tiger?
Yes, it is. / No, it isn't.

❸ Is it an elephant?
Yes, it is. / No, it isn't.

❹ Is it a pencil case?
Yes, it is. / No, it isn't.

❺ Is it a window?
Yes, it is. / No, it isn't.

THINK AGAIN!

A famous animal from China is the _____.

My favorite lesson is on page _____.

A traditional costume from China is the _____.

WORKBOOK page 19   **STICKERS**   **PASSPORT** page 4

USA

National Aeronautics and Space Administration (NASA).

A newspaper headline about the Apollo 11 landing.

Neil Armstrong, Michael Collins, and Buzz Aldrin, Apollo 11 astronauts.

Apollo 11 lunar lander.

STEAM

TEAM NAME

Do you want to go to the moon? Why?

1 Get materials.

cardboard box

small paper cup

large marshmallows

scissors

duct tape

construction paper

Additional materials:

cotton balls

styrofoam pieces

tinfoil

biodegradable straws

bubble wrap

2 pairs of cleaning gloves

cling film

Super Star Challenge

The International Space Station is a science lab in space.

Russian astronaut Valentina Tereshkova was the first woman in space.

30

CHALLENGE 1

LAND ON THE MOON

CHINA

China National Space Administration (CNSA).

2 Design a safe moon lander. Look at some examples:

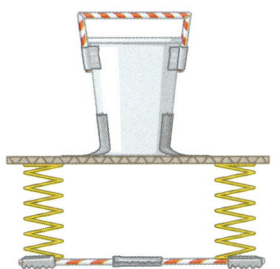
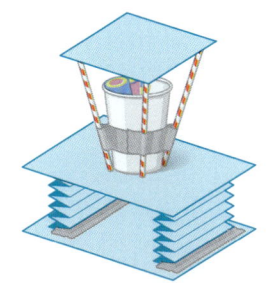

3 Test your design.

The launch of the Chang'e 4 lander and rover mission from the Xichang launch center, in China.

4 Draw your best design.

Chinese Chang'e 4 lunar lander.

Is the moon a good place to build a colony?

Super Star Challenge
Build an astronaut's glove box.

Chinese Yutu 2 lunar rover.

 TEAMWORK

31

Unit 3

Lesson 1 · VOCABULARY·

TRACK 22

1 Listen, point, and say.

one   two   three   four   five

six   seven   eight   nine   ten

TRACK 23

2 Listen, count, and say.

3 Play the Make Ten Game.

Six.

And four.

Ten!

WORKBOOK page 20

Lesson 2

GRAMMAR
How old are you? I'm seven.

 TRACK 24

1 Listen and read.

2 Number the words.

◯ old ① How ◯ you? ◯ are ◯ six. ◯ I'm

3 Ask and answer.

WORKBOOK page 21

GRAMMAR GUIDE page 130

Lesson 3

·SOUNDS GREAT·

 **1** Listen and chant.

Ten big pens in a big box.

 2 Listen and say.

ten   big   pen   box

3 Look, listen, and connect.

1 🖊   p   n
              e
2 📦   b   x
              o
3 🔟   t   n
              e
4 🐱   b ⌒⌒⌒ g
              i

 **4** Read the chant and underline *e*, *i*, *p*, and *b*.

Lesson **4**

READING TIME

TRACK 28

1 Listen and read.

1
- What's in the big box?
- It's my birthday cake.

2
- How old are you?
- I'm seven.

3
- It's my birthday.
- It's his birthday, too.

4
- Happy birthday!
- Woof!
- Thank you!

2 Read the story again. Check (✓) the **value**.

It's good to share. ◯   Celebrate your birthday. ◯

3 Read and circle.

I share with my **mom** / **dad** / **brother** / **sister** / **friend** / **dog**.

WORKBOOK page 23

37

Unit 3 — Lesson 5

VOCABULARY

TRACK 29

1 Listen, point, and say.

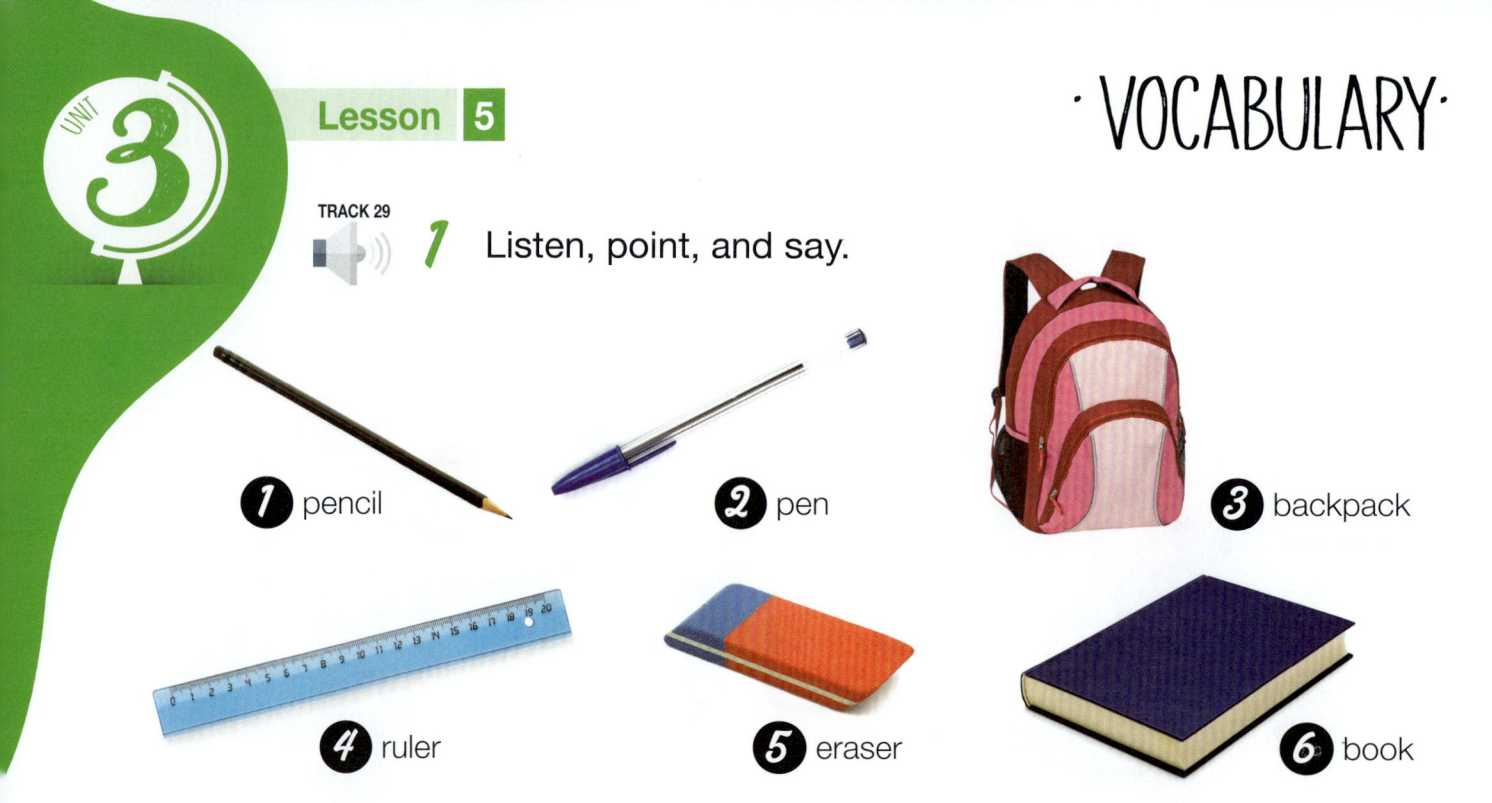

1. pencil
2. pen
3. backpack
4. ruler
5. eraser
6. book

2 Look at Activity 1. Point, ask, and answer.

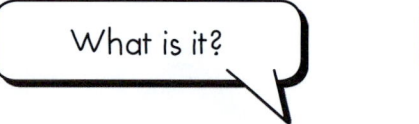

> What is it?

> It's a book.

TRACK 30

3 Sing and act. **Counting Song**.

Pick up a pencil,
Pick up a pen,
Pick up a book,
And count to 10!
1, 2, 3, 4, 5, 6,
7, 8, 9, 10!

Pick up a backpack,
Pick up a pen,
Pick up an eraser,
And count to 10!
1, 2, 3, 4, 5, 6,
7, 8, 9, 10!

WORKBOOK page 24

Lesson 6

GRAMMAR
One book. Two book**s**.
One pen. Three pen**s**.

TRACK 31

1 Listen, read, and say.

One, two, three, four, five, six pencils.

One, two, three, four books.

2 Look at Activity 1 and circle.

1 two pens — True / False
2 three backpacks — True / False
3 three erasers — True / False

3 Look at Activity 1. Play the Counting Game.

Erasers!

One, two, three.

WORKBOOK page 25

GRAMMAR GUIDE page 130

UNIT 3 — Lesson 7 — FUN READER

LET'S VISIT RUSSIA

1 Read about traditional objects from Russia.

Hi, I'm Alex. I'm seven years old, and I'm from Russia. This is a traditional costume from my country. It's beautiful!

Look! Eight colored eggs.

Look! Five colored dolls.

Think Twice

1 Cover the text and write.

_____ eggs.

_____ dolls.

2 Circle the traditional object you prefer.

Lesson 8

SPEAKING TIME

1 Draw a traditional toy from your country.

NEW FRIENDS

1 Complete the conversation. Choose your response.

This is a toy from _____.

Let's play.

No, thank you. ○

OK. Good idea! ○

2 Act out the conversation.

WORKBOOK page 26

SPAIN

WELCOME
15 JULY
SPAIN
40°26'N 3°42'W
UTC+2

Welcome to Spain!

Look! A dancer.

UNIT 4

TRACK 32

🔊 **Listen and check (✓).**

1 💃 ○   2 💃 ○

UNIT 4

Lesson 1

VOCABULARY

TRACK 33

1 Listen, point, and say.

1. teacher
2. actor 
3. doctor 
4. farmer 
5. cook 
6. artist 

TRACK 34

2 Listen and guess.

3 Play the Guessing Game.

Farmer!

WORKBOOK page 27

44

Lesson 2

GRAMMAR

His name's Hercule. **He's a** cook.
Her name's Mary. **She isn't a** cook.

TRACK 35

1 Listen and read.

"His name's Hercule. He's a cook. Her name's Mary. She isn't a cook. She's a doctor."

2 Choose and circle.

1 **He's** / **She's** a cook.

2 He **'s** / **isn't** a cook.

3 He **'s** / **isn't** an artist.

3 Point and say.

"She's a ...
She isn't a ..."

WORKBOOK page 28

GRAMMAR GUIDE page 130

UNIT 4

Lesson 3

SOUNDS GREAT

TRACK 36

1 Listen and chant.

Is it a fox with seven sisters?
No!
Is it a fox with six sisters?
Yes!

TRACK 37

2 Listen and say.

s   y   f   x

sister   yes   fox   six

TRACK 38

3 Look, listen, and connect.

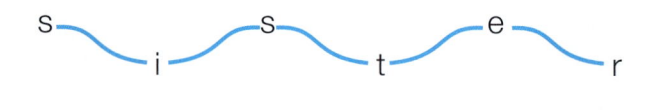

1  s — i — s — t — e — r

2  f   x
      o

3 y   s
      e

4 s   x
      i

4 Read the chant and underline *s*, *y*, *f*, and *x*.

WORKBOOK page 29

Lesson 4

READING TIME

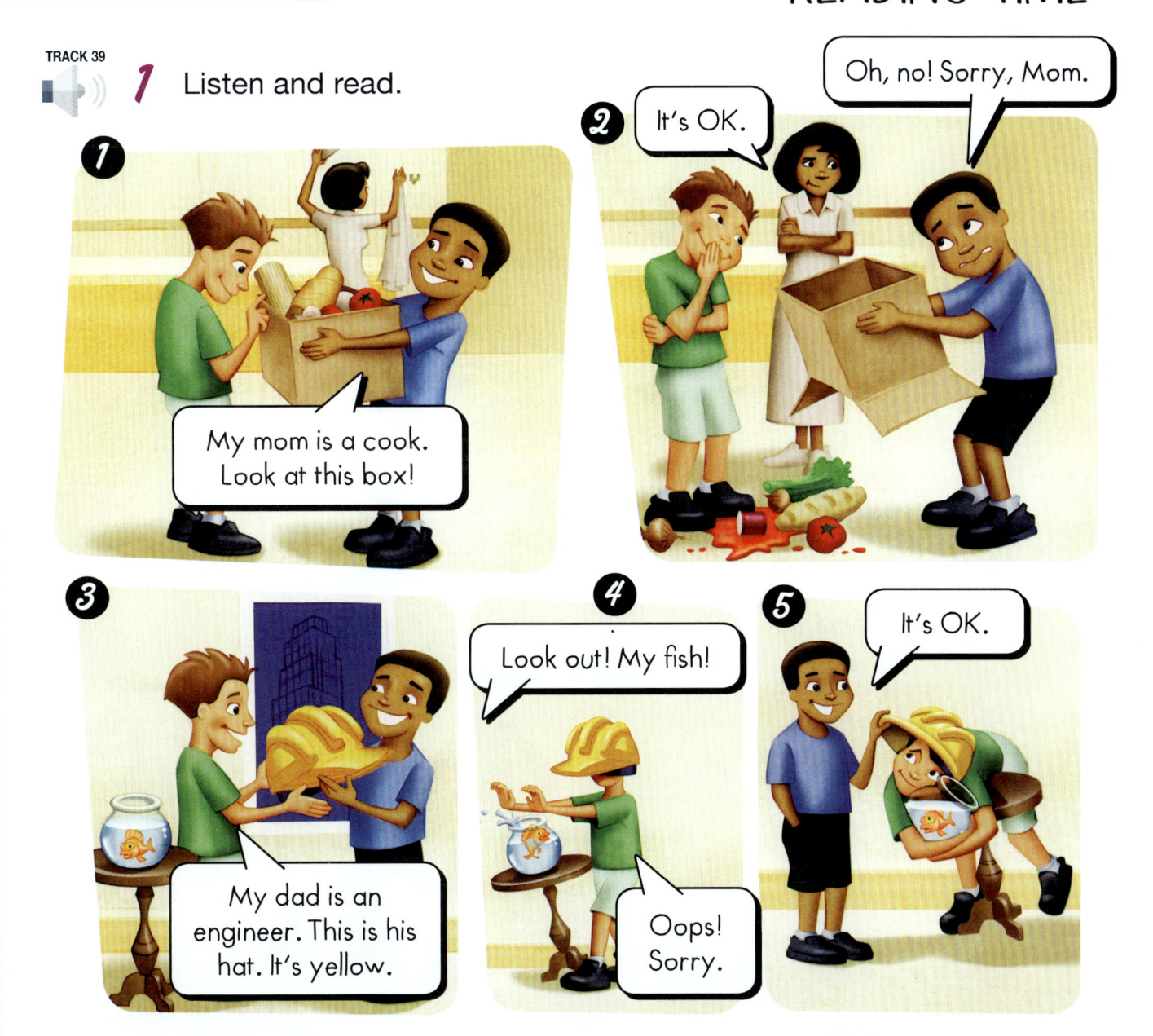

1 Listen and read.

1 My mom is a cook. Look at this box!

2 It's OK. Oh, no! Sorry, Mom.

3 My dad is an engineer. This is his hat. It's yellow.

4 Look out! My fish! Oops! Sorry.

5 It's OK.

2 Read the story again. Check (✓) the **value**.

Accept apologies. ◯   Be careful. ◯

3 How do you feel when you are sorry? Circle.

happy / sad

WORKBOOK page 30

47

UNIT 4

Lesson 5

·VOCABULARY·

TRACK 40

1 Listen, point, and say.

1 singer
2 dancer
3 taekwondo instructor
4 engineer
5 inventor
6 soccer player

2 Match and say.

1 He's a soccer player.
2 He's a taekwondo instructor.
3 He's a singer.

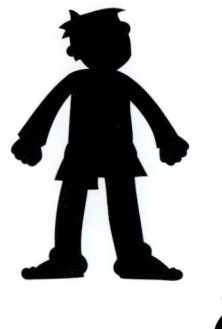

3 Draw, write, and say.

He's a soccer player. His name's …

WORKBOOK page 31

48

Lesson 6

GRAMMAR
Is he a dancer / **an** actor?
Yes, **he is**. / No, **he isn't**.

TRACK 41

1 Listen, read, and say.

- Look! Is she an actor?
- Is she a dancer?
- No, she isn't.
- Yes, she is.

TRACK 42

2 Sing. **Working People**

Is he an artist?
Is he an actor?
No, no, no, he isn't.
Is he a farmer with a big, red tractor?
Yes, yes, yes, he is!

Is she a singer?
Is she a cook?
No, no, no, she isn't.
Is she a teacher with a big, green book?
Yes, yes, yes, she is!

WORKBOOK page 32

GRAMMAR GUIDE page 130

UNIT 4 — Lesson 7

FUN READER

LET'S VISIT SPAIN

1 Read about working people from Spain.

Hi! I'm Laura. This is my dad, Juan. He's a cook. He's in his restaurant.

Look at the delicious paella! Paella is a traditional dish from Spain.

This is my mom, Fernanda. She's an artist. She's a good painter, but she isn't famous. Her favorite artist is Pablo Picasso. Picasso is a very famous artist from Spain. His paintings are in the Picasso Museum in Malaga.

Think Twice

1 Circle the one that doesn't belong.
   a cook / restaurant / artist
   b painter / paella / museum

2 Name a famous person in your country. What's his / her job?

Lesson 8

SPEAKING TIME

1 Draw a traditional dish from your country and write.

This is _____.
It's a traditional dish from my country.

NEW FRIENDS

1 Complete the conversation. Choose your response.

This is _____.
It's a traditional dish from my country. Try it!

Thanks! It's delicious. ○

No, thanks. ○

2 Act out the conversation.

WORKBOOK page 33

PROGRESS CHECK

UNIT 3

✓ **1** Count, write, and say.

1 I'm _____. 2 I'm _____. 3 I'm _____.

✓ **2** Count and circle.

1 one book / three books
2 one ruler / six rulers
3 one backpack / two backpacks
4 one pencil / four pencils
5 one eraser / two erasers

THINK AGAIN!

A traditional object from Russia is _____.

My favorite picture is on page _____.

My favorite lesson is on page _____.

52

WORKBOOK page 34   **STICKERS**   **PASSPORT** page 6

UNIT 4 · PROGRESS CHECK ·

✓ 1 Check (✓) and say.

1. He's ○ / She's ○ a singer.
2. He's ○ / She's ○ a cook. 
3. He's ○ / She's ○ a soccer player. 
4. He's ○ / She's ○ a farmer. 

✓ 2 Match.

1. Is he an inventor? — Yes, he is.
2. Is she a dancer? — Yes, she is.
3. Is she a cook? — No, he isn't.
4. Is he an engineer? — No, she isn't.

THINK AGAIN!

A famous dish from Spain is _____.

My favorite lesson is on page _____.

A famous person from Spain is _____.

WORKBOOK page 35 · **STICKERS** · **PASSPORT** page 8

RUSSIA

Woman wearing a folk costume.

Matryoshka dolls, big and small.

Nesting of opened *matryoshka*.

STEAM

TEAM NAME

What is folk art?

1 Get materials.

- 3 construction paper squares
- 3 construction paper circles 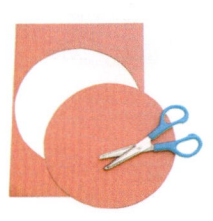
- glue 
- colored markers 
- 2 cardboard strips
- 4 metal bottle caps 

Super Star Challenge

Matryoshkas, castanets, and guitars are made of wood.

54

CHALLENGE 2

MAKE CRAFT MATRYOSHKAS

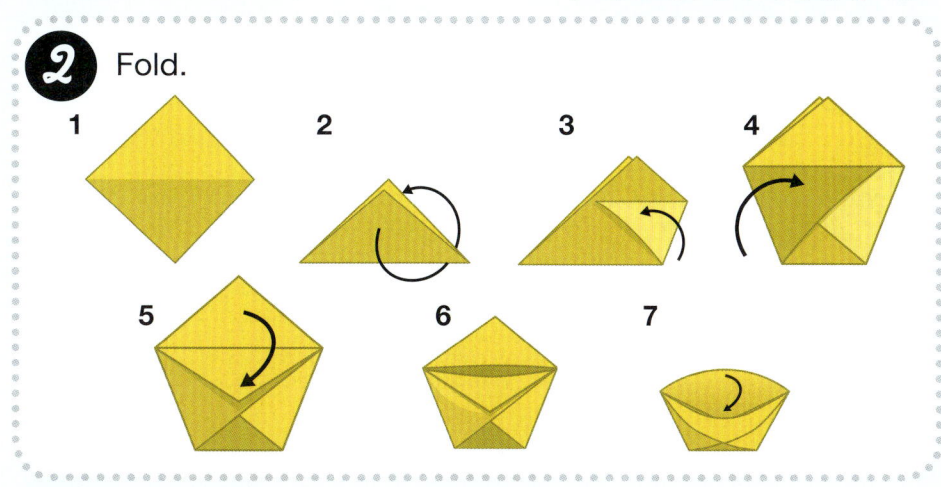

2 Fold.

1 2 3 4
5 6 7

3 Glue, decorate, and play.

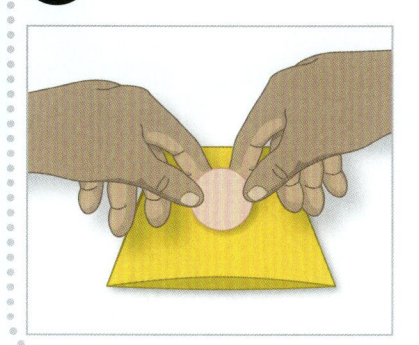

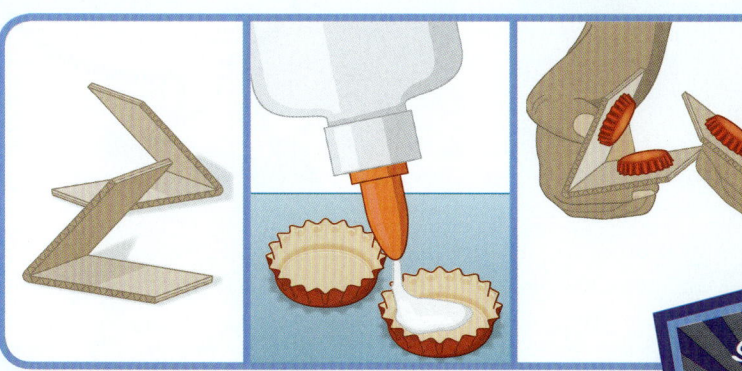

What folk art is your country famous for?

Super Star Challenge
Make craft castanets.

SPAIN

A flamenco dancer wearing traditional clothing.

A tradition for all ages.

Castanets are used in classical and folk dances.

TEAMWORK

55

EGYPT

UNIT 5

Welcome to Egypt!

Look at the camel.

✓ Count the colors on the camel.

UNIT 5

Lesson 1

·VOCABULARY·

1 Listen, point, and say.

1. doll
2. computer game
3. teddy bear
4. robot
5. bike
6. kite

2 Listen and circle.

1. kite / bike
2. robot / doll
3. teddy bear / computer game
4. robot / bike

3 Draw, ask, and answer.

Is it a kite?

Is it a teddy bear?

No, it isn't.

Yes, it is.

WORKBOOK page 36

Lesson 2

GRAMMAR
What **are** they?
They**'re** bikes.

TRACK 45

1 Listen, read, and say.

What are they?
They're robots.

2 Look, read, and circle.

What is it? / What are they?

They're dolls. / They're bikes. / They're robots.

TEMPLATE 5

3 Complete, color, and play.

What are they?
They're robots.
No. They're dolls.

WORKBOOK page 37

GRAMMAR GUIDE page 131

59

UNIT 5 · SOUNDS GREAT ·

Lesson 3

TRACK 46

1 Listen and chant.

I am a queen
and this is my kite.
My kite is red and green.

Wow! It's windy.
Quick! My kite!
Oh, no! It's in a tree.

TRACK 47

2 Listen and say.

w   k   g   q   r

windy   kite   green   queen   red

TRACK 48

3 Look, listen, and connect.

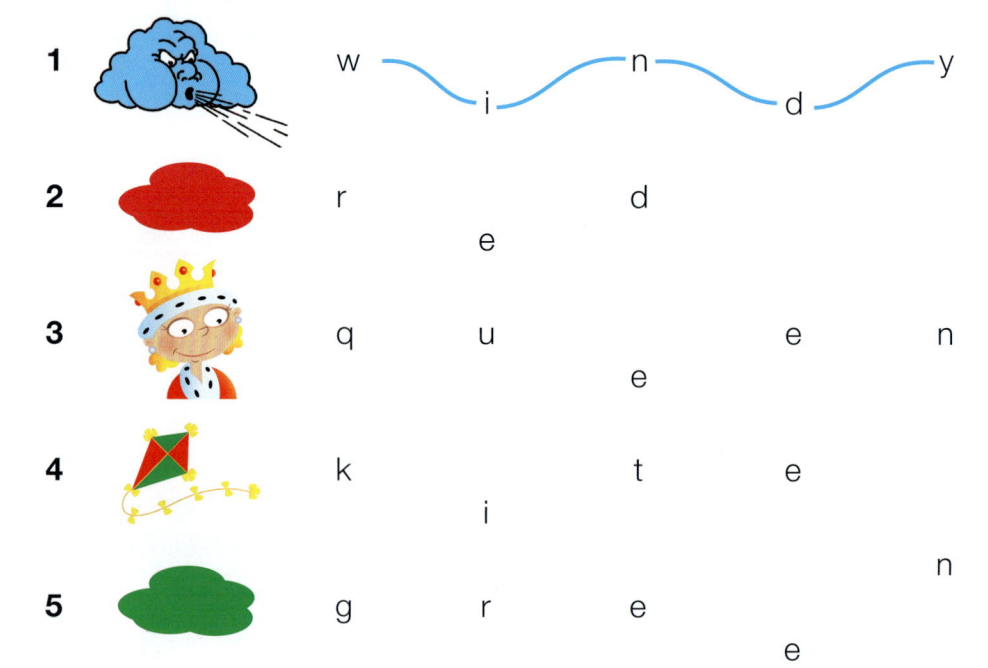

1. w — i — n — d — y

2. r   d
      e

3. q   u   e   n
         e

4. k   t   e
      i
            n

5. g   r   e
         e

4 Read the chant. Underline *w*, *k*, *g*, *q*, and *r*.

WORKBOOK page 38

60

Lesson 4

READING TIME

TRACK 49

1 Listen and read.

1. What are they?
They're my teddy bears and robots.

2. Here you are. Let's play together.
Thank you.

3. Wow! It's windy.
Quick! Here's a kite.

4. A red kite for you and a green kite for me.

2 Read the story again. Check (✓) the **value**.

Play together. ○   Be helpful. ○

3 Read and circle.

I play with my **mom** / **dad** / **sister** / **brother** / **friends**.

WORKBOOK page 39

61

UNIT 5 — Lesson 5

VOCABULARY

TRACK 50

1 Listen, point, and say.

1. gray
2. yellow
3. white
4. green
5. red
6. blue
7. pink
8. black
9. orange
10. brown

TRACK 51

2 Listen and color. Which color is missing?

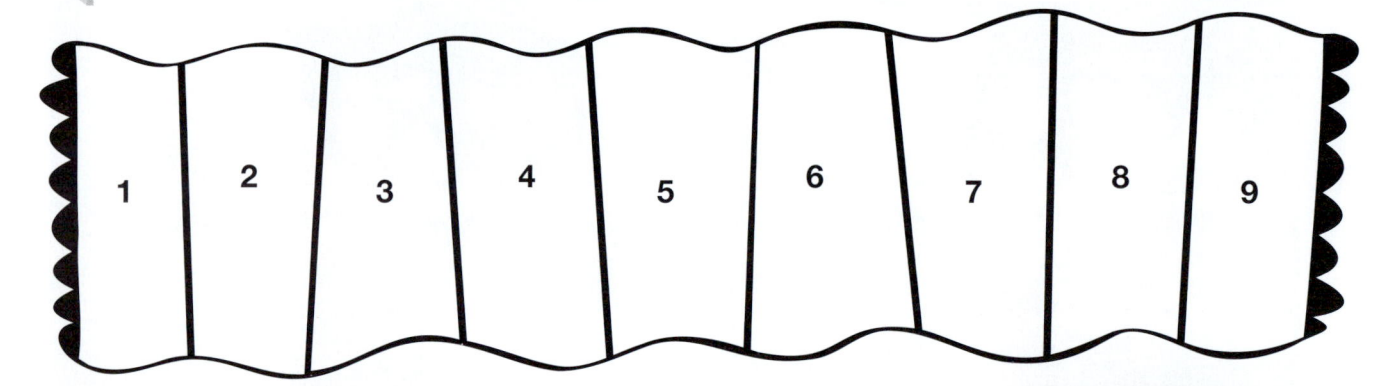

1 2 3 4 5 6 7 8 9

3 Talk about your things.

"This is my pencil case. It's red."

WORKBOOK page 40

Lesson 6

GRAMMAR
Are they yellow?
Yes, **they are.** / No, **they aren't.**

TRACK 52

1 Listen, read, and say.

Are they black?

No, they aren't.

Are they yellow?

Yes, they are.

Oh, yes! Wow!

TRACK 53

2 Sing. **Teddy Bears For You!**

Are they green teddy bears?
No, they aren't. No, they aren't.

Are they blue teddy bears?
No, they aren't. No, they aren't.

Are they yellow teddy bears?
Yes, they are. Yes, they are.

The teddy bears are yellow
They aren't green or blue,
The teddy bears are yellow
And they are for you!

WORKBOOK page 41

GRAMMAR GUIDE page 131

Lesson 7 — FUN READER

LET'S VISIT EGYPT

1 Read about a famous place in Egypt.

Hi, I'm Azibo. Look at these pictures of Egypt.

What is it?

It's one of the pyramids at Giza, in Egypt. They're very popular with tourists.

Look! It's a decorated camel. Look at the colors. The camel is brown and its decorations are red, white, black, yellow, orange, green, and blue. The camels at Giza are very famous and they're very popular with tourists at the pyramids!

Think Twice

1 Read and circle.
Camels are at the pyramids.
True / False

2 Which animals are popular in your country?

Lesson 8

SPEAKING TIME

1 Draw a famous place in your country.

NEW FRIENDS

1 Complete the conversation. Choose your response.

_____ is a famous place in my country.

It looks interesting. ○

It's beautiful. ○

2 Act out the conversation.

WORKBOOK page 42

65

MEXICO

MEXICO

Welcome to Mexico!

UNIT 6

Look! It's a jaguar!

Which animal isn't from Mexico? Circle.

UNIT 6 Lesson 1 · VOCABULARY ·

TRACK 54

1 Listen, point, and say.

PET SHOW

1 bird
2 dog
3 cat
4 turtle
5 rabbit
6 horse

2 Read and circle.

1 It's a (cat) / dog.

2 It's a **bird** / **turtle**.

3 It's a **rabbit** / **horse**.

3 Draw, color, write, and say.

TEMPLATE 6

It's a yellow bird.

WORKBOOK
page 43

68

Lesson 2

GRAMMAR

I **have** a cat.
I **don't have** a dog.

TRACK 55

1 Listen, read, and say.

"I have a dog."

"I don't have a dog. I have a cat and a horse!"

2 Write *have* or *don't have*.

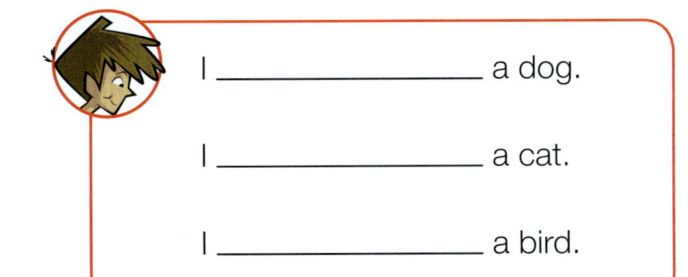

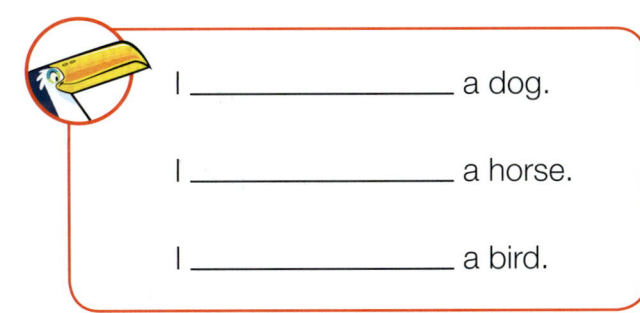

I _____ a dog.
I _____ a cat.
I _____ a bird.

I _____ a dog.
I _____ a horse.
I _____ a bird.

3 Tell a friend about yourself.

a cat   a dog   a red pencil
a fish   a panda   a tiger   a teddy bear

"I don't have a dog. I have a cat."

"I have a cat. I don't have a dog."

WORKBOOK page 44

GRAMMAR GUIDE page 131

UNIT 6 — Lesson 3

SOUNDS GREAT

TRACK 56

1 Listen and chant.

> At night a van is at the zoo.
> With a lion, a zebra, and a jaguar, too.

TRACK 57

2 Listen and say.

| l | j | z | v | n |

lion   jaguar   zebra   van   night

TRACK 58

3 Look, listen, connect, and write.

1. z
2. j
3. n
4. v
5. l

____ aguar

____ ion

____ an

____ ebra

____ ight

4 Read the chant and underline *l*, *j*, *z*, *v*, and *n*.

WORKBOOK page 45

Lesson 4

READING TIME

TRACK 59

1 Listen and read.

1 This is my pet. His name's Jazz. He has nine spots. He isn't a jaguar, but he's a cat!

2 I love you very much, Jazz.

Meow!

3 This is his bed, and this is his bowl.

4 Good night, Jazz.

2 Read the story again. Check (✓) the value.

Be kind to your pet. ○   Love animals. ○

3 Which animal is a good pet for your family? Circle.

WORKBOOK page 46

71

UNIT 6

Lesson 5

VOCABULARY

TRACK 60

1 Listen, point, and say.

1 snake

2 iguana

3 spider

4 hamster

5 mouse

6 frog

TRACK 61

2 Listen and circle.

1 spider / snake
2 mouse / frog
3 iguana / hamster
4 iguana / spider

3 Talk to a friend.

I have a mouse.

I don't have a spider.

WORKBOOK
page 47

72

Lesson 6

GRAMMAR
Do you have a dog?
Yes, I do. / No, I don't.

TRACK 62

1 Listen, read, and say.

- Do you have a frog?
- No, I don't.
- Do you have a spider?
- Yes, I do.

TRACK 63

2 Sing. **Do You Have a Pet?**

Do you have a cat? Do you have a frog?
Do you have a fish? Do you have a dog?
Yes, I do! Yes, I do! Yes, I do! Yes, I do!

Do you have a rabbit? Do you have a spider?
Do you have a hamster? Do you have a tiger?
No, I don't! No, I don't! No, I don't! No, I don't!

3 Ask and answer.

- Do you have a frog?
- No, I don't.

WORKBOOK page 48

GRAMMAR GUIDE page 131

Unit 6 — Lesson 7

FUN READER

LET'S VISIT MEXICO

1 Read about exotic pets in Mexico.

Hello! I'm Sara. I'm eight years old, and I'm from Sonora, in Mexico.

I have a fantastic pet! This is Charlie, my iguana. Charlie is a beautiful green color. I love my iguana!

I also have a big spider called a tarantula. Her name's Betty, and she's from Mexico. She's orange and black. My pets are great! Do you have a pet?

Think Twice

1. How many pets does Sara have?
2. Which pet do you like? Circle.

   spider / iguana

Lesson 8

SPEAKING TIME

1 Draw, write, and say.

This is my exotic pet. His / Her name is _____.

NEW FRIENDS

1 Complete the conversation. Choose your response.

My favorite animal is my iguana.

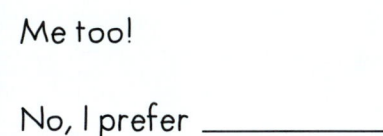

Me too! ○

No, I prefer _____! ○

2 Act out the conversation.

WORKBOOK page 49

PROGRESS CHECK

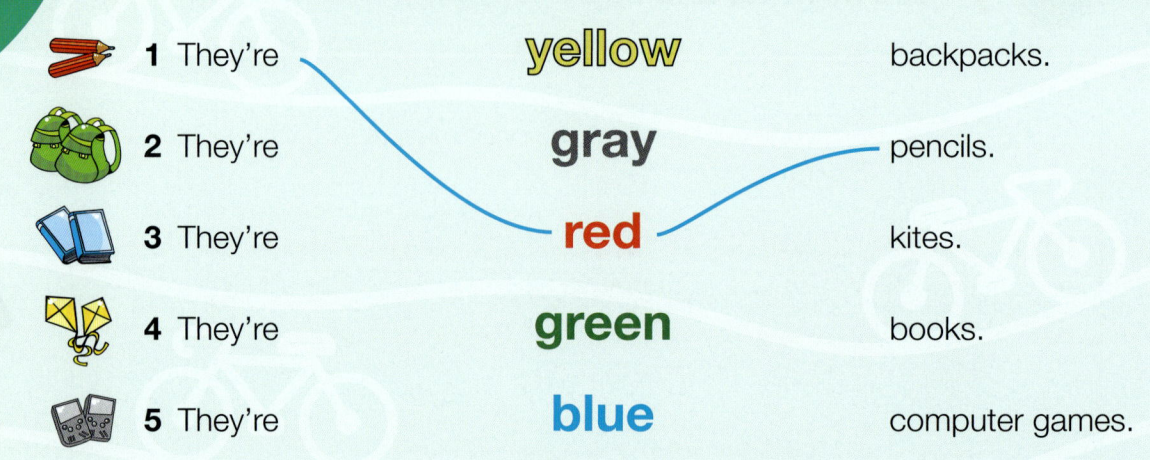

UNIT 5

✓ **1** Connect and say.

1 They're   yellow   backpacks.
2 They're   gray   pencils.
3 They're   red   kites.
4 They're   green   books.
5 They're   blue   computer games.

✓ **2** Look at Activity 1. Check (✓).

	Yes, they are.	No, they aren't.
1 Are they blue pencils?	○	○
2 Are they green backpacks?	○	○
3 Are they pink books?	○	○
4 Are they yellow kites?	○	○
5 Are they red computer games?	○	○

THINK AGAIN!

A famous place in Egypt is _____.

My favorite picture is on page _____.

A typical animal from Egypt is _____.

WORKBOOK page 50   **STICKERS**   **PASSPORT** page 10

PROGRESS CHECK

1 Circle to make true sentences for you.

1. I   have / don't have   a brother.
2. I   have / don't have   a sister.
3. I   have / don't have   a turtle.
4. I   have / don't have   a computer game.

2 Look at Activity 1. Ask and answer.

Do you have a brother?

Yes, I do.

3 Look in your pencil case. Match.

1. Do you have a red pen?   Yes, I do.
                              No, I don't.

2. Do you have two erasers?   Yes, I do.
                              No, I don't.

3. Do you have a ruler?   Yes, I do.
                              No, I don't.

THINK AGAIN!

An animal from Mexico is _____.

My favorite lesson is on page _____.

A place in Mexico is _____.

WORKBOOK page 51   **STICKERS**   **PASSPORT** page 12

EGYPT

The Great Pyramid of Giza, a wonder of the ancient world.

The Step Pyramid, the oldest in Egypt.

Egyptian hieroglyphs.

STEAM

TEAM NAME

Pyramids are very impressive structures. What do you know about them?

1 Get materials.

- plastic cups
- rubber band 
- 4 pieces of string 
- permanent markers 

2 Tie the strings to the rubber band and make a tool.

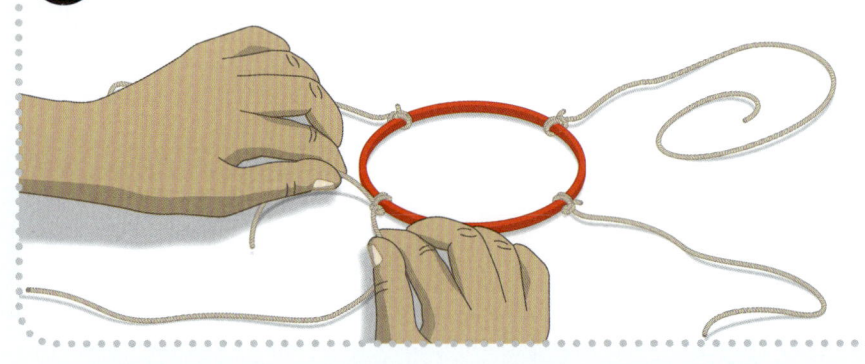

Hieroglyphic writing uses pictures as symbols.

The Egyptians and Mayans used hieroglyphs on their temple walls and monuments.

CHALLENGE 3

·BUILD A PYRAMID·

MEXICO

3. Decorate the cups with Mayan or Egyptian hieroglyphs.

4. Grab a string. Work together to move the cups to build a pyramid.

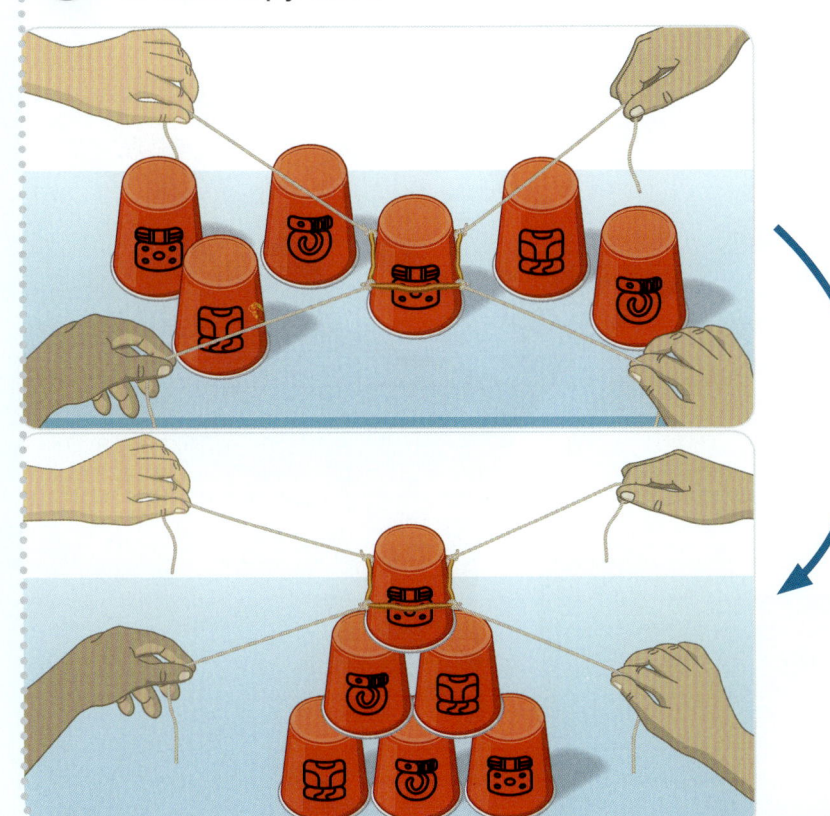

Do you know any building that looks like a pyramid?

The Pyramid of Kukulkan at the Mayan ruins of Chichen Itza.

The Pyramid of the Sun in Teotihuacan.

Mayan hieroglyphs.

Super Star Challenge
Build a pyramid with more cups.

TEAMWORK

INDIA

INDIA
Taj Mahal
INDIA

Welcome to India!

UNIT 7

Look at her black eyes.

Look at the picture. Guess her job.

actor   dancer   teacher

UNIT 7 — Lesson 1 · VOCABULARY·

TRACK 64

1 Listen, point, and say.

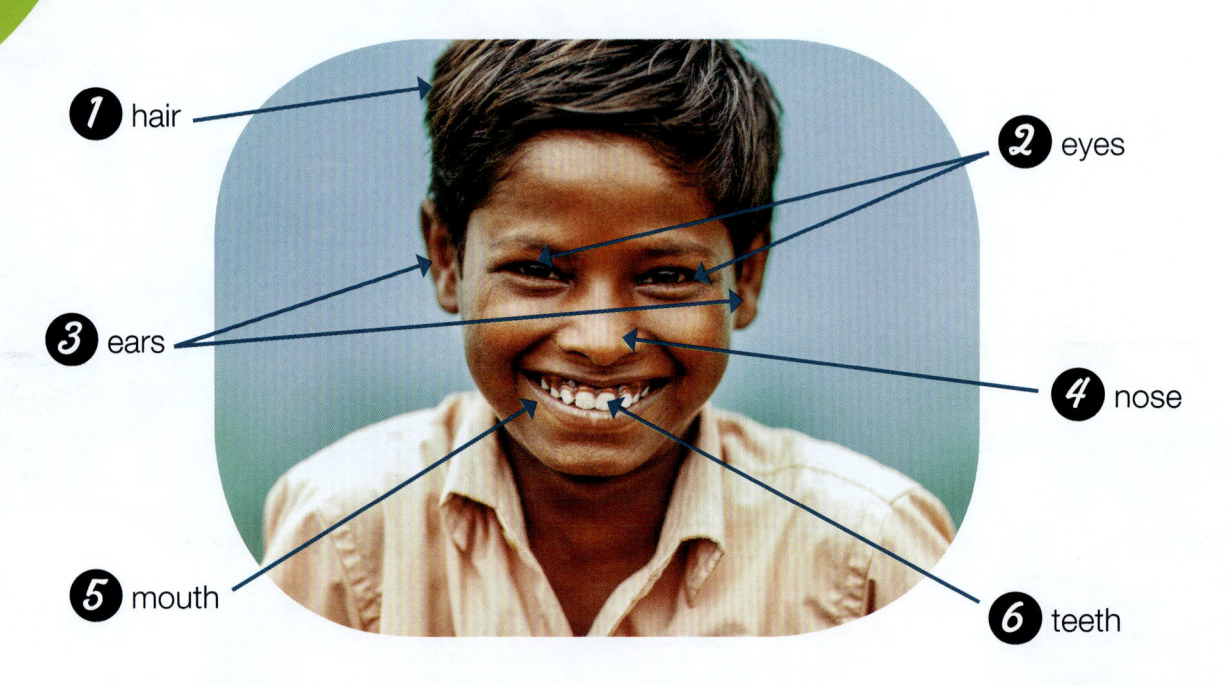

1. hair
2. eyes
3. ears
4. nose
5. mouth
6. teeth

TRACK 65

2 Listen and do.

3 Play the Touch Game.

Touch your hair!

WORKBOOK page 52

Lesson 2

GRAMMAR
He has black hair.
She has blue hair.

TRACK 66

1 Listen and read.

Look! He has black hair and she has blue hair!

No! She has black hair. Look!

TRACK 67

2 Listen and say *True* or *False*.

3 Make a friend and say.

TEMPLATE 7

Paco has brown hair.

WORKBOOK page 53

GRAMMAR GUIDE page 132

83

UNIT 7 — Lesson 3

SOUNDS GREAT

TRACK 68

1 Listen and chant.

> Hello, doll. Look at me.
> I'm a black and yellow bee.
> Buzz, buzz, buzz. Look at me.
> I'm a dizzy, dizzy bee.

TRACK 69

2 Listen and say.

ll **zz**

hello   doll   yellow   dizzy   buzz

TRACK 70

3 Listen and write *ll* and *zz*.

di____y   bu____   do____   ye____ow

4 Read the chant and underline *ll* and *zz*.

WORKBOOK page 54

84

Lesson 4 ·READING TIME·

TRACK 71

1 Listen and read.

1 This is my doll. Her name's Bella. Wash your face, Bella.

2 Brush your hair.

3 Brush your teeth.

4 Lizzy, wash your face and brush your hair, please.

2 Read the story again. Check (✓) the value.

Be clean. ◯   Take care of your toys. ◯

3 Read and circle.

I brush my teeth. / I wash my face. / I brush my hair.

WORKBOOK page 55

85

UNIT 7

Lesson 5

VOCABULARY

TRACK 72

1 Listen, point, and say.

1. hands
2. arms
3. legs
4. feet
5. fingers
6. toes

2 Look at the alien and say.

> He has six toes.

TRACK 73

3 Sing and act. **Happy Body Song**

Shake your arms,
Shake your legs,
Clap your hands,
And stamp your feet.

Arms, legs, hands, feet!
Arms, legs, hands, feet!

Touch your ears,
Touch your toes,
Close your eyes,
And touch your nose.

Ears, toes, eyes, nose!
Ears, toes, eyes, nose!

WORKBOOK page 56

Lesson 6

GRAMMAR

Does she have two eyes?
Yes, **she does**. / No, **she doesn't**.

TRACK 74

1 Listen, read, and say.

- Does it have four legs?
- No, it doesn't.
- Does it have eight legs?
- Yes, it does.
- It's a spider!

2 Look and circle.

1. Does she have two noses?
Yes, she does. / No, she doesn't.

2. Does he have two mouths?
Yes, he does. / No, he doesn't.

3. Does it have two eyes?
Yes, it does. / No, it doesn't.

3 Play the Guessing Game.

- Does he have blond hair?
- Yes, he does.
- It's Mark!

WORKBOOK page 57

GRAMMAR GUIDE page 132

87

Lesson 7 · FUN READER ·

LET'S VISIT INDIA

1 Read about dancers in India.

This is Amla. She's fourteen years old.

Is she an actor?

No, she isn't. She's a traditional dancer from India. She's a very good dancer, and she's very popular with tourists. She has a beautiful traditional costume – it's pink, blue, and gray. Look at the position of her arms, legs, and hands. It's very difficult to be a good dancer!

Think Twice

1 Circle.
It is / It isn't difficult to be a good dancer.

2 Do you have a traditional costume?

Lesson 8

SPEAKING TIME

1 Draw, write, and say.

This is a traditional costume from India.

This is a traditional costume from _____.

NEW FRIENDS

1 Complete the conversation. Choose your response.

This is a traditional costume from _____.

It's similar to our traditional costume. ○

It's different from our traditional costume. ○

2 Act out the conversation.

WORKBOOK page 58

UK

Unit 8

Welcome to the UK!

Look! A guard and a castle.

Look and check (✓).
Is it Buckingham Palace or the Tower of London?

UNIT 8

Lesson 1

VOCABULARY

TRACK 75

1 Listen, point, and say.

1. pool
2. park 
3. mall 
4. stadium 
5. school 
6. zoo 

TRACK 76

2 Listen and guess.

3 Act and say.

It's a pool!

WORKBOOK page 59

Lesson 2

GRAMMAR

There's a pool.
There isn't a stadium.

TRACK 77

1 Listen, read, and say.

Look! There's a park and a zoo.

There isn't a pool or a mall.

2 Look at Activity 1. Write *There's* or *There isn't*.

1 ____There's____ a bike.
2 _____ a ball.
3 _____ a turtle.
4 _____ an elephant.

3 Draw and say.

In my town, there isn't a zoo. There's a pool.

WORKBOOK page 60

GRAMMAR GUIDE page 132

93

Unit 8

Lesson 3

SOUNDS GREAT

TRACK 78

1 Listen and chant.

> A giraffe in a dress,
> in the grass, on a cliff.

TRACK 79

2 Listen and say.

ss **ff**

grass   dress   cliff   giraffe

TRACK 80

3 Listen and write *ss* and *ff*.

cli____    gra____    dre____    gira____e

4 Read the chant and underline *ss* and *ff*.

WORKBOOK page 61

Lesson 4 ·REEADING TIME·

TRACK 81

1 Listen and read.

1 Jeff and Cassie are in the park.

Look! There's litter on the grass.

What a mess!

2 Jeff and Cassie make signs.

Throw Your Litter in the Trash Can

KEEP OFF THE GRASS

3 Don't drop litter on the grass. Throw it in the trash can.

4 There isn't litter in the park now!

2 Read the story again. Check (✓) the **value**.

Don't drop litter. ◯   Work together. ◯

3 Read and circle.

I **drop** / **don't drop** litter.

WORKBOOK page 62

95

UNIT 8

Lesson 5

VOCABULARY

TRACK 82

1 Listen, point, and say.

① tree
② river
③ beach
④ mountain
⑤ flower
⑥ lake

TRACK 83

2 Listen and complete.

1 It's a _____.
2 It's a _____.
3 It's a _____.
4 It's a _____.

TRACK 84

3 Sing. **Way Up High**.

Fly, fly up to the sky,
Look at the world,
From way up high.

I see mountains,
I see trees,
I see a lake,
And a yellow beach.

I see a park,
I see a river,
I see you,
And a red flower.

96

WORKBOOK
page 63

Lesson 6

GRAMMAR

Is there a river?
Yes, **there is**. / No, **there isn't**.

TRACK 85

1 Listen, read, and say.

- Is there a river?
- Yes, there is.
- Is there a zoo?
- No, there isn't.

2 Look at Activity 1 and play the Memory Game.

a zoo   a park   a lake   a stadium   a mountain

- Is there a zoo?
- No, there isn't.

WORKBOOK page 64

GRAMMAR GUIDE page 132

UNIT 8

Lesson 7

FUN READER

LET'S VISIT THE UK

1 Read about favorite places in the UK.

This is Tommy. He's from England, and this is his favorite place. It's a castle. It's very old.

This is Sally, and this is her favorite place. It's a park. It's beautiful.

Look! There's a lake. Is there a beautiful park in your neighborhood?

Think Twice

1 Match the favorite places.
Tommy — a park
Sally — a castle

2 Which place do you prefer? The castle or the park?

Lesson 8

SPEAKING TIME

1 Draw and write.

This is a special place. It's called _____.

NEW FRIENDS

1 Complete the conversation. Choose your response.

My favorite place is a castle.

It looks fun. ○
It looks boring. ○

2 Act out the conversation.

WORKBOOK page 65

UNIT 7 · PROGRESS CHECK

1 Look and circle.

1 He has / She has / It has   brown eyes.
2 He has / She has / It has   blue eyes.
3 He has / She has / It has   blond hair.
4 He has / She has / It has   four legs.
5 He has / She has / It has   black hair.
6 He has / She has / It has   a robot.

2 Look at Activity 1 and underline.

1 Does she have a bike?
   Yes, she does. / No, she doesn't.
2 Does he have a robot?
   Yes, he does. / No, he doesn't.
3 Does it have a teddy bear?
   Yes, it does. / No, it doesn't.

3 Look at Activity 1. Ask and answer.

Does she have brown eyes?   Yes, she does.

THINK AGAIN!

The colors of Amla's traditional Indian costume are: _____.
_____.
My favorite picture is on page _____.
_____ are very popular with tourists in India.

WORKBOOK page 66   STICKERS   PASSPORT page 14

PROGRESS CHECK

1 Connect to make true sentences.

1 In my classroom …

There's
There isn't

a clock.
a window.
a door.
a bike.

2 In my town …

There's
There isn't

a stadium.
a pool.
a lake.
a zoo.

2 Look and check (✓).

1 Is there an elephant?
Yes, there is. ◯   No, there isn't. ◯

2 Is there a snake?
Yes, there is. ◯   No, there isn't. ◯

3 Is there a spider?
Yes, there is. ◯   No, there isn't. ◯

4 Is there an iguana?
Yes, there is. ◯   No, there isn't. ◯

5 Is there a monkey?
Yes, there is. ◯   No, there isn't. ◯

THINK AGAIN!

_____ is a castle in the UK.

My favorite lesson is on page _____.

My favorite place in the UK is _____.

WORKBOOK page 67   **STICKERS**   **PASSPORT** page 16

INDIA

Cows are sacred animals in India.

Indian farmer milking a cow by hand.

Ghee, Indian clarified butter.

STEAM

TEAM NAME

Name 5 things made with milk.

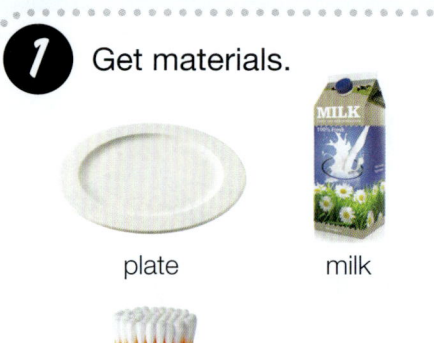

1 Get materials.

- plate
- milk
- food coloring
- dish soap
- cotton swabs
- watercolor paper

Super Star Challenge

2 Pour milk onto the plate.

Dish soap is a kind of detergent. We can use it to clean dishes, clothes, houses, etc.

Excessive use of detergents causes water and soil pollution.

CHALLENGE 4

· COLOR CHANGING MILK ·

UNITED KINGDOM

3 Add drops of food coloring.

4 Dip cotton swab into milk.

5 Drop dish soap onto dry cotton swab. Then dip it into milk.

What causes the different reactions in steps 4 and 5?

Super Star Challenge
Make paper for cards or bookmarks.

Scottish Highland cow.

Woman on a dairy farm in Wales.

Stilton, a popular British cheese.

TEAMWORK ★★★★☆

BRAZIL

BRAZIL

Welcome to Brazil!

UNIT 9

Look at the fruits.

Circle the fruits you eat.

UNIT 9

Lesson 1

VOCABULARY

1 Listen, point, and say.

TRACK 86

1. pineapple
2. banana 
3. watermelon 
4. orange 
5. apple 
6. pear 

2 Draw, color, and write.

TEMPLATE 9

3 Sing. **Amazing Mrs. Fruity**

TRACK 87

Hello, hello, hello, Mrs. Fruity,
How are you? How are you?

Apples, oranges, and pineapples, too,
Look at you, look at you.
Bananas, pears, watermelons, too,
Look at you, look at you.

Hello, hello, hello, Mrs. Fruity,
How are you? How are you?

WORKBOOK page 68

Lesson 2

TRACK 88

1 Listen, read, and say.

> GRAMMAR
> **There's** one banana.
> **There are** three pears.

- There are three bananas and two pears.
- There's one watermelon.
- Oops! There isn't a watermelon now.

Banana
Pear
Pineapple
Orange
Watermelon
Apple

2 Look at Activity 1. Write *There's* or *There are*.

1 _____ one pineapple.

2 _____ six oranges.

3 Talk to a friend.

- In my picture, there are three oranges.
- In my picture, there are four oranges.

WORKBOOK page 69

GRAMMAR GUIDE page 133

107

UNIT 9 — Lesson 3 · SOUNDS GREAT ·

TRACK 89

1 Listen and chant.

What's in the shopping cart?
A chicken and some chips,
peaches, cherries, and a fish.

TRACK 90

2 Listen and say.

ch   **sh**

chicken   peach   shopping cart   fish

TRACK 91

3 Listen and write *ch* and *sh*.

fi_____   _____opping cart   pea_____   _____icken

4 Read the chant and underline *ch* and *sh*.

108

WORKBOOK page 70

Lesson 4

READING TIME

TRACK 92

1 Listen and read.

1 Shelly is at the grocery store. She has cherries and peaches in her shopping cart.

2 Mmm ... I like cherries.

3 Josh! They aren't your cherries.

4 Your cherries. Sorry!
Thank you.

2 Read the story again. Check (✓) the **value**.

Eat fruit. ◯   Don't take others' things. ◯

3 Look at picture 4. Imagine you're Josh. Circle.

I feel **good** / **bad**.

WORKBOOK page 71

109

UNIT 9

Lesson 5

VOCABULARY

TRACK 93

1 Listen, point, and say.

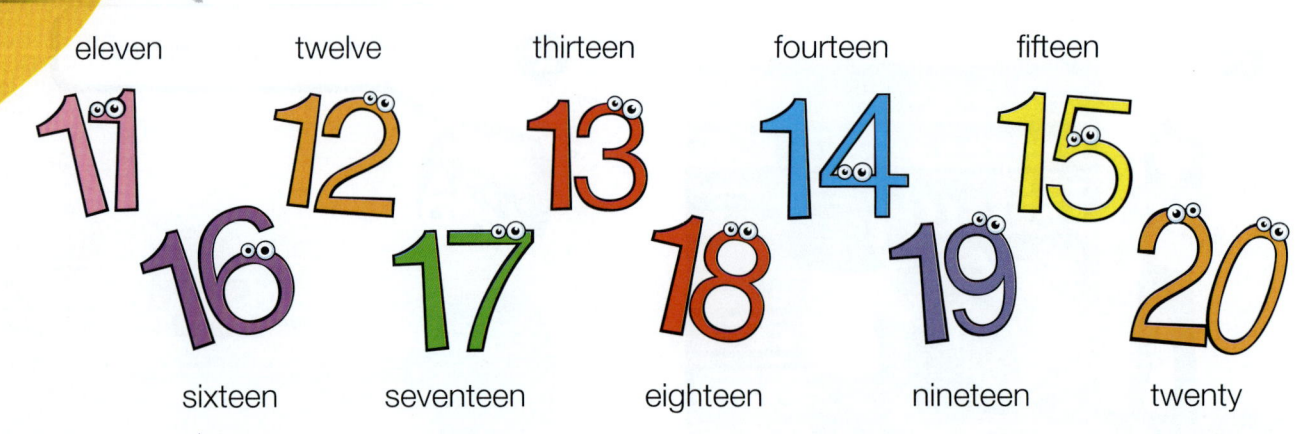

| eleven | twelve | thirteen | fourteen | fifteen |

11 12 13 14 15

16 17 18 19 20

| sixteen | seventeen | eighteen | nineteen | twenty |

TRACK 94

2 Listen, count, and say.

3 Count, write, and say.

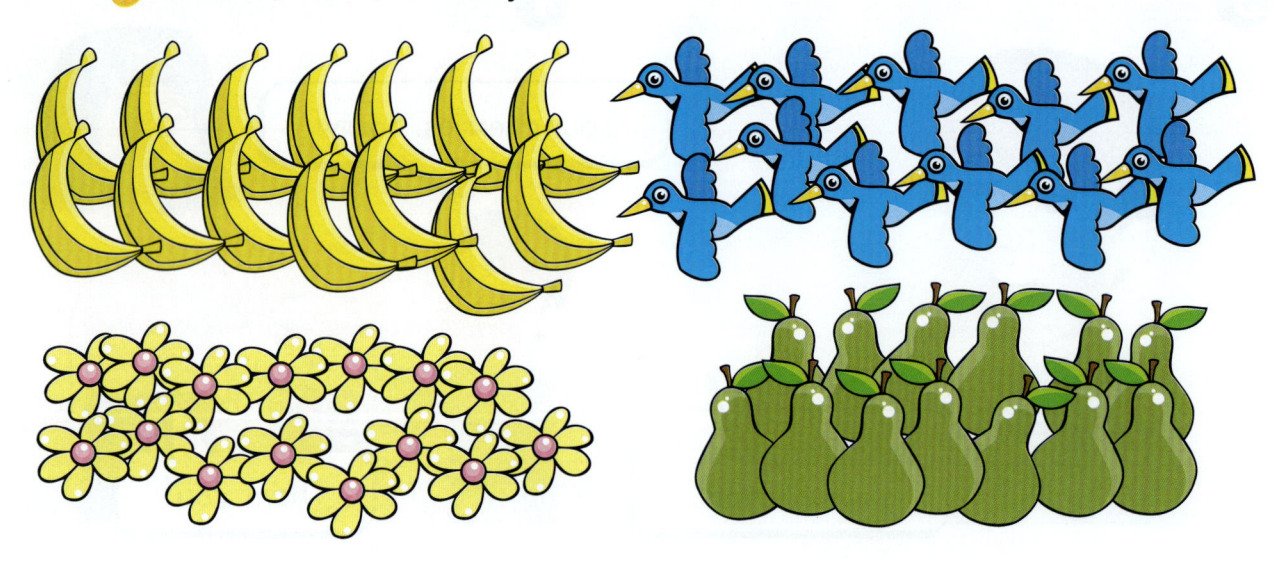

1 There are _____fourteen_____ bananas.

2 There are _____ flowers.

3 There are _____ birds.

4 There are _____ pears.

> There are fourteen bananas.

WORKBOOK page 72

110

Lesson 6

GRAMMAR

How many bananas **are there?**
There are twelve.

TRACK 95

1 Listen, read, and say.

How many bananas are there?

There are twelve bananas.

How many oranges are there?

There are eleven oranges.

2 Complete, ask, and answer.

In your classroom …

1 How _____ windows are there?

There are _____ _____.

2 How many girls _____ there?

There are _____ _____.

3 How many boys are _____?

There are _____ _____.

How many windows are there?

There are …

WORKBOOK page 73

GRAMMAR GUIDE page 133

Unit 9 Lesson 7 · FUN READER ·

LET'S VISIT BRAZIL

1 Read about fruits in Brazil.

This is Ana from the Amazon rainforest in Brazil. She is nine years old. In the rainforest, there are lots of delicious fruits. Some are bananas, pineapples, and papayas.

Papayas are very popular in Brazil. Papayas are orange, and they have black seeds. Are there papayas in your country?

Think Twice

1 Circle.
Papayas are black, and they have orange seeds.

True / False

2 Check (✓). Papayas are delicious.

Yes ◯   No ◯

Lesson 8

SPEAKING TIME

1 Draw, color, write, and say.

_____ and _____ are fruits from my country.

NEW FRIENDS

1 Complete the conversation. Choose your response.

_____ and _____ are my favorite fruits.

They're my favorite, too. ○

I prefer _____. ○

2 Act out the conversation.

WORKBOOK page 74

113

JAPAN

JAPAN

UNIT 10

Welcome to Japan!

Look at this family and their house!

Who is missing? Check (✓).

mom ○ grandpa ○

UNIT 10

Lesson 1

VOCABULARY

TRACK 96

1 Listen, point, and say.

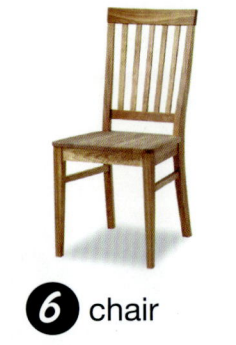

1. table
2. closet
3. TV
4. bed
5. sofa
6. chair

2 Talk to a friend.

There isn't a closet.

There's a sofa.

WORKBOOK page 75

Lesson 2

GRAMMAR

The book is **in / on / under** the backpack.

TRACK 97

1 Listen, read, and say.

OK. The teddy bear is on the bed. The book is under the chair. The kite is in the closet.

Let's go out!

2 Look at Activity 1 and write.

1 The robot is _____ the table.
2 The pencil case is _____ the backpack.
3 The ball is _____ the bed.

TRACK 98

3 Listen, act, and say.

The pen is on the book.

WORKBOOK page 76

GRAMMAR GUIDE page 133

UNIT 10

Lesson 3

SOUNDS GREAT

1 Listen and chant.

Thank you for the pink cupcakes.
Thank you for the juice.
Thank you for the things you do.
I sing this song for you.

2 Listen and say.

nk   **ng**

pink   thank   thing   sing

3 Listen and write *nk* and *ng*.

s i ___ ___   p i ___ ___   t h a ___ ___

4 Read the chant and underline *nk* and *ng*.

WORKBOOK page 77

118

Lesson 4

READING TIME

TRACK 102

1 Listen and read.

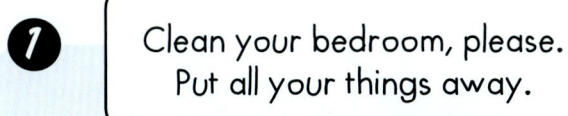

1 Clean your bedroom, please. Put all your things away.

2 My toys are in the box.

3 And my books are on the table.

4 All *my* things are neat, Mom.

Thank you.

2 Read the story again. Check (✓) the **value**.

Be neat. ◯   Listen to your mom. ◯

3 Look at picture 4. Imagine you're the boy. Circle.

I will help my mom.   Yes / No

WORKBOOK page 78

119

UNIT 10

Lesson 5

· VOCABULARY ·

TRACK 103

1 Listen and repeat.

1. bathroom
2. bedroom
3. kitchen
4. living room
5. garage
6. yard

TRACK 104

2 Listen and guess.

3 Draw and say.

This is my house. The bed is in the bedroom. The book is ...

WORKBOOK page 79

120

Lesson 6

TRACK 105

1 Listen, read, and say.

GRAMMAR

Where's the cat?
It's in / on / under the closet.
Where are the birds?
They're in / on / under the tree.

Where's the cat?

It's in the yard.

Where are the birds?

They're in the tree. Quick!

2 Complete the sentences.

1 _____ the cat?

_____ in the yard.

2 _____ the chairs?

_____ in the kitchen.

3 Look at Activity 1. Play the Memory Game.

Where's the table?

It's in the yard.

No.

It's in the kitchen.

WORKBOOK page 80

GRAMMAR GUIDE page 133

121

UNIT 10 · Lesson 7 — FUN READER

LET'S VISIT JAPAN

1 Read about a house in Japan.

Hi! I'm Etsu, and I'm from Osaka, in Japan.

This is my house. We have two bedrooms, a bathroom, a living room, a kitchen, and a garden. Gardens are very popular in Japan. This is a picture of our traditional garden. There are trees, but there aren't flowers. Look at the stones! It's beautiful here. Do you have a garden?

Think Twice

1. How many rooms are there in Etsu's house?
2. Imagine you're in the garden.

   I can see _____.
   I can hear _____.

Lesson 8

SPEAKING TIME

1. Draw, color, write, and say.

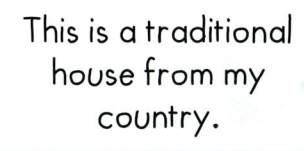

This is a traditional house from my country.

NEW FRIENDS

1. Complete the conversation. Choose your response.

Welcome to my home!

Thank you. ◯
This is nice. ◯

2. Act out the conversation.

WORKBOOK page 81

123

PROGRESS CHECK

UNIT 9

✓ **1** Look and check (✓).

	Picture 1	Picture 2
1 There's one pear.	○	○
2 There are six apples.	○	○
3 There are eight bananas.	○	○
4 There's one pineapple.	○	○
5 There are five oranges.	○	○
6 There are four watermelons.	○	○

✓ **2** Look at Activity 1. Ask and answer.

> How many pears are there?

> There's one pear.

✓ **3** Count and write.

1 _____ pears.

2 _____ apples.

3 _____ bananas.

THINK AGAIN!

_____ is a fruit from Brazil.

A place I connect with Brazil is _____.

My favorite picture is on page _____

WORKBOOK page 82   STICKERS   PASSPORT page 18

UNIT 10 · PROGRESS CHECK·

✓ **1** Look, write, ask, and answer.

| in | on | under |

1 The bed is _____in_____ the bedroom.

2 The pen is _____ the table.

3 The teddy bear is _____ the closet.

4 The ball is _____ the chair.

5 The cat is _____ the bed.

6 The book is _____ the table.

Where's the teddy bear?

It's in the closet.

✓ **2** Look and check (✓).

1 Where's the doll?

It's in the closet. ◯   It's on the sofa. ◯

2 Where are the flowers?

They're on the table. ◯   They're in the yard. ◯

3 Where's the sofa?

It's in the living room. ◯   They're in the living room. ◯

THINK AGAIN!

_____ are very popular in Japan.

My favorite lesson is on page _____.

My favorite picture is on page _____.

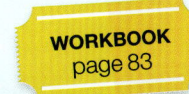

WORKBOOK page 83   **STICKERS**   **PASSPORT** page 20

BRAZIL

Interlagos racetrack, Sao Paulo, Brazil.

Ayrton Senna, Formula 1 champion from Brazil.

Ayrton Senna's Formula 1 car.

STEAM

TEAM NAME

Name objects with an axle.

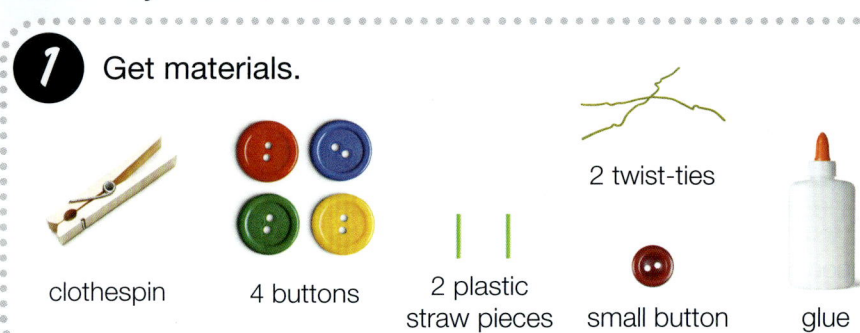

1 Get materials.

- clothespin
- 4 buttons
- 2 plastic straw pieces
- 2 twist-ties
- small button
- glue

2 Build 2 axles with button wheels.

1 2 3 4

The wheel and axle help to move heavy loads. They rotate together when a force is applied to either of them.

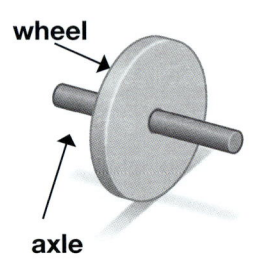

wheel
axle

We see the wheel and axle in many other things.

wheelbarrow   steering wheel

CHALLENGE 5

·RACE A CAR·

JAPAN

3 Attach wheels.

1 2

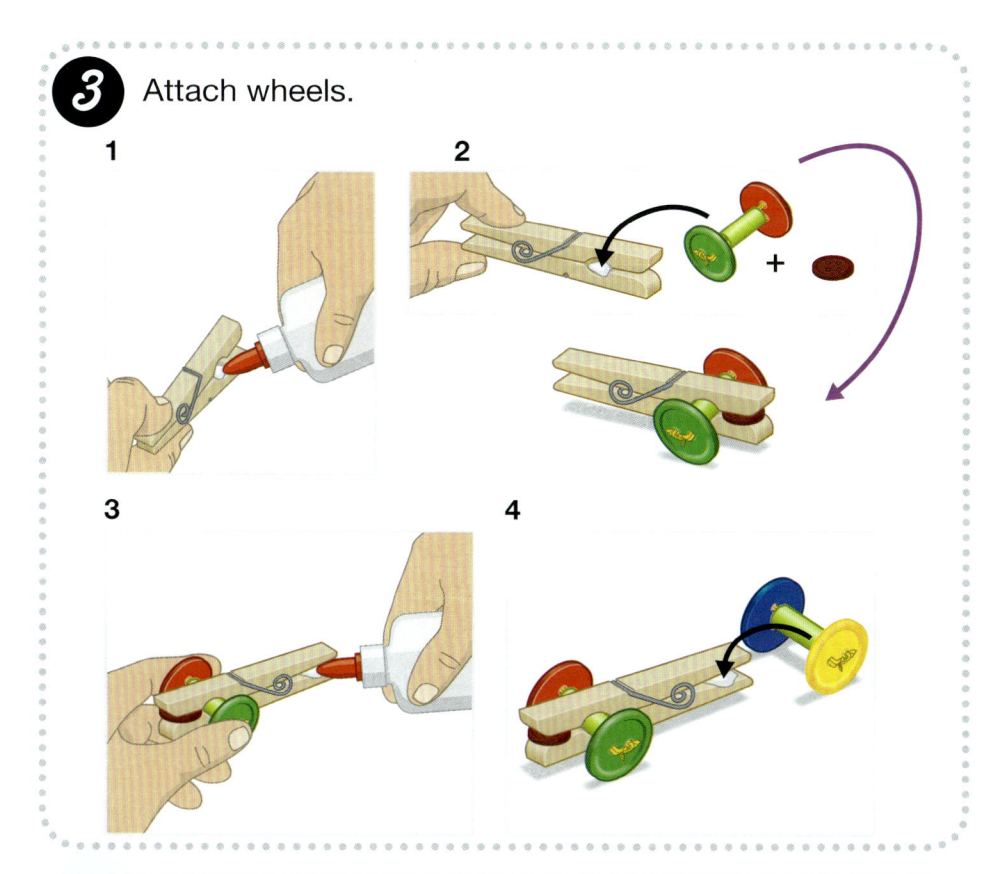

3 4

4 Test drive your car!

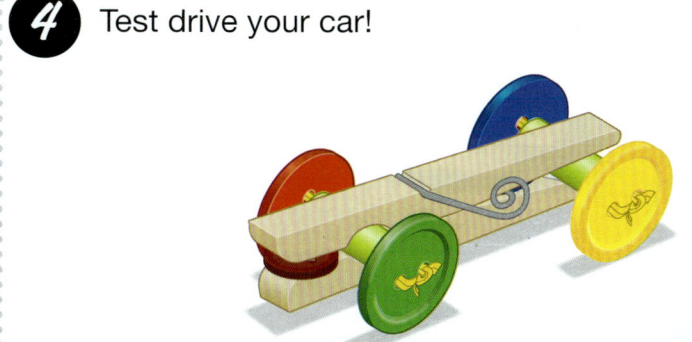

Solve the problem: 10 teams each enter 2 cars into the Formula 1 World Championship. How many drivers will race?

Super Star Challenge

Build a racetrack.

Suzuka racetrack, Suzuka city, Japan.

Kamui Kobayashi, a race car driver from Japan.

Kamui Kobayashi's Formula 1 car.

TEAMWORK ★★★★☆

127

GRAMMAR GUIDE

HOW TO USE THE GRAMMAR GUIDE

Hello! I'm Grant. I'm your Grammar Guide. I love grammar! Come and see me after each grammar lesson. I'm here to help you. Follow me!

GRANT'S HOME STUDY GUIDE

1. Read your Grammar Guide again at home.
2. Look at the example. Close your book. Try to say the example.
3. Open your book and check.

1 After your grammar lessons, turn to the Grammar Guide. Look at the example.

What's your name?
My name's Grant. = **I'm** Grant.

2 Complete the activity.

1. Complete.
   What's your ____name____?
   My _____.

3. Check your answers.

Come back and see me if you get lost!

UNIT 1 USA

Lesson 2

What's your name?
My name's Grant. = **I'm** Grant.

Complete.
What's your _____?
My _____.

Lesson 6

This is my mom.

Complete.
_____ my mom.
_____ my dad.

UNIT 2 CHINA

Lesson 2

What is it?
It's a monkey.
It's an octopus.
(an + a, e, i, o, u)

Complete.
1. What is it?
   It's _____ tiger.
2. What is it?
   It's _____ elephant.
3. What is it?
   It's _____ octopus.

Lesson 6

Is it a window?
No, **it isn't**.
Is it a door?
Yes, **it is**.

Complete.
Is it a clock?
Yes, _____.
No, _____.

UNIT 3 RUSSIA

Lesson 2

How old are you?
I'm six. (**I'm** = **I am**)

Complete.

How _____ are _____?

I'm _____.

Lesson 6

One ruler.
Three book**s**.

Look in Grant's bag. Complete.

One _____.

Two _____.

Three _____.

UNIT 4 SPAIN

Lesson 2

Her name's Maria.
His name's Grant.
She isn't a teacher.
She's a dancer.
He's a guide.

Complete.

1 _____ a guide.

2 _____ a teacher.

3 _____ name's Grant.

4 She's a _____.

Lesson 6

Is she a dancer?
Yes, **she is**.
Is she an artist?
No, **she isn't**.

Complete.

1 Is Grant a guide?
   Yes, _____.

2 Is Maria an artist?
   No, _____.

3 Is Grant a farmer?
   No, _____.

4 Is Maria a dancer?
   Yes, _____.

UNIT 5 EGYPT

Lesson 2

What are they?
They're kites.

Complete.

1. What _____ they?

   They're bikes.

2. What are they?

   _____ dolls.

3. _____

   They're robots.

Lesson 6

Are they blue? Yes, **they are.**
Are they green? No, **they aren't.**

Complete.

1. Are they yellow kites?

   No, _____.

2. Are they blue dolls?

   Yes, _____.

UNIT 6 MEXICO

Lesson 2

I have a horse.
I don't have a dog.

Complete to make true sentences about you.

1. I _____ a dog.

2. I _____ a cat.

3. I don't have a _____.

Lesson 6

Do you have a horse? Yes, **I do.**
Do you have a dog? No, **I don't.**

Complete.

1. _____ you have a tiger?

   No, I _____.

2. Do you _____ a fish?

   Yes, I _____.

UNIT 7 INDIA

Lesson 2

He has brown eyes. **She has** green hair.

Complete.

1 He _____ brown hair.
2 She _____ blue eyes.
3 _____ has green hair.
4 _____ has brown eyes.

Lesson 6

Does she have blond hair?
No, **she doesn't**.
Does she have brown hair?
Yes, **she does**.

Complete.

1 _____ she have brown hair?
   Yes, she _____.
2 Does it _____ four legs?
   No, it _____.

UNIT 8 UK

Lesson 2

There's a park. **There isn't** a zoo.

Complete. Write about your town.

1 _____ a pool.
2 _____ a mall.
3 _____ a zoo.

Lesson 6

Is there a lake? Yes, **there is**.
Is there a mountain? No, **there isn't**.

Complete. Write about your town.

1 _____ there a beach?
   _____.
2 Is _____ a zoo?
   _____.
3 Is there a _____?
   Yes, there _____.

132

UNIT 9 BRAZIL

Lesson 2

There's one watermelon.
There are seven oranges.

Complete. Write about the fruits in the picture.

1 There _____ five bananas.
2 _____ _____ nine apples.
3 There _____ one pineapple.

Lesson 6

How many apples **are there?**
There are nine apples.

Complete.

1 How _____ oranges are there?
2 There _____ eleven pears.
3 How many pineapples _____ there?

UNIT 10 JAPAN

Lesson 2

The TV is **in** the closet. (**in/on/under**)

Complete.

1 The backpack is _____ the chair.
2 The TV is _____ the closet.
3 The books are _____ the bed.

Lesson 6

Where's the TV? **It's in** the closet.
Where are the books? **They're on** the bed.

Complete.

1 Where _____ the spider?
_____ under the chair.
2 _____ _____ the books?
They're on the bed.
3 _____ the TV?
_____ in the closet.

133

2020 © Macmillan Education do Brasil

Based on *Next Move*
© Macmillan Publishers Limited 2013
Text © Cantabgilly Limited and Mary Charrington 2013
Adapted by Viv Lambert
Grammar Guide written by Viv Lambert
STEAM Challenge sections written by Sarah Elizabeth Sprague
Next Move is a registered trademark, property of Macmillan Publishers, 2013
First edition entitled "Next Stop" published 2009 by Macmillan Publishers

Director of Languages Brazil: Patrícia Souza De Luccia
Publishing Manager and Field Researcher: Patricia Muradas
Content Creation Coordinator: Cristina do Vale
Art Editor: Jean Aranha
Lead Editors: Ana Beatriz da Costa Moreira, Daniela Gonçala da Costa, Luciana Pereira da Silva
Content Editors: Millyane M. Moura Moreira, Tarsílio Soares Moreira
Digital Editor: Ana Paula Girardi
Editorial Assistant: Roberta Somera
Editorial Intern: Bruna Marques
Art Assistant: Denis Araujo
Art Intern: Jacqueline Alves
Graphic Production: Tatiane Romano, Thais Mendes P. Galvão
Proofreaders: Edward Willson, Márcia Leme, Sabrina Cairo Bileski
Design Concept: Design Divertido Artes Gráficas
Page Make-Up: Figurattiva Editorial
Photo Research: Marcia Sato
Image Processing: Jean Aranha, Jacqueline Alves
Audio: Argila Music, Núcleo de Criação
Cover Concept: Jean Aranha
Cover photography: CasarsaGuru/iStockphoto/Getty Images, Bubert/iStockphoto/Getty Images, LokFung/iStockphoto/Getty Images.
Commissioned photography: Macmillan Publishers Ltd/Paul Bricknell (p. 10, 15, 20, 21, 25, 34, 35, 44, 48, 58, 59, 62, 68, 82, 83, 87, 92, 93, 97, 106, 117, 120, 121).
Map: Allmaps
Illustrations: Adilson Secco (p. 30-31, 55, 78-79, 102-103, 126-127), Rita Gianetti (p. 20, 28, 29, 49, 52, 53, 59, 63, 68, 70, 77, 87, 96, 101, 124, 125), Anna Godwin | Beehive Illustration (p. 12, 22, 36, 46, 60, 70, 84, 94, 108, 118), David Harrington Studio Inc (p. 13, 23, 37, 47, 61, 71, 85, 95, 109, 119), David Hurtado (p. 132), Andrew Painter | Beehive Illustration (p. 4, 10, 11, 15, 21, 25, 35, 39, 46, 49, 59, 63, 69, 73, 83, 87, 93, 97, 107, 111, 117, 121), Jim Peacock | Beehive Illustration (p. 22, 29, 34, 52, 48, 62, 73, 86, 87, 100, 107, 110, 120), Anthony Rule (p. 128, 129, 130, 131, 132, 133).

Reproduction prohibited. Penal Code Article 184 and Law number 9.610 of February 19, 1998.

We would like to dedicate this book to teachers all over Brazil. We would also like to thank our clients and teachers who have helped us make this book better with their many rich contributions and feedback straight from the classroom!

The authors and publishers would like to thank the following for permission to reproduce the photographic material:
p. 8: Bullit Marquez/Ap Images/Glow Images; p. 14: laflor/iStockphoto/Getty Images, Jakovos/iStockphoto/Getty Images; p. 16: kate_sept2004/iStockphoto/Getty Images, McIninch/iStockphoto/Getty Images, Richard T. Nowitz/Getty Images; p. 18: gangliu10/iStockphoto/Getty Images; p. 24: koya79/iStockphoto/Getty Images, onebluelight/iStockphoto/Getty Images, Nerthuz/iStockphoto/Getty Images, Matthew71/iStockphoto/Getty Images, PhonlamaiPhoto/iStockphoto/Getty Images, zaptik/iStockphoto/Getty Images, Wavebreakmedia/iStockphoto/Getty Images; p. 26: Image Source/iStockphoto/Getty Images, fototrav/iStockphoto/Getty Images, hanhanpeggy/iStockphoto/Getty Images; p. 27: Alamy/Fotoarena; p. 30: MargaretClavell/iStockphoto/Getty Images, Pgiam/iStockphoto/Getty Images, Kalulu/iStockphoto/Getty Images, NASA Images, EASEP/Nasa, STS-116 Shuttle Crew/NASA, Sovfoto/UIG/Easypix,stphillips/iStockphoto/Getty Images, karandaev/iStockphoto/Getty Images, Devonyu/iStockphoto/Getty Images, natthanim/iStockphoto/Getty Images, Devonyu/iStockphoto/Getty Images, nortongo/iStockphoto/Getty Images; p. 31: Ismailciydem/iStockphoto/Getty Images, China National Space Administration, China National Space Administration/China News Service/Getty Images, China National Space Administration/China News Service/Getty Images, xenicx/iStockphoto/Getty Images, rclassenlayouts/iStockphoto/Getty Images, clubfoto/iStockphoto/Getty Images, EHStock/iStockphoto/Getty Images, alenkadr/iStockphoto/Getty Images, philipimage/iStockphoto/Getty Images; p. 32: ollikainen/iStockphoto/Getty Images; p. 38: AndreaAstes/iStockphoto/Getty Images, pamela_d_mcadams/iStockphoto/Getty Images, Dmitriy Kazitsyn/iStockphoto/Getty Images, boygovideo/iStockphoto/Getty Images, studiocasper/iStockphoto/Getty Images, seb_ra/iStockphoto/Getty Images, belchonock/iStockphoto/Getty Images; p. 40: Sergey Ryumin/Getty Images, BrankoPhoto/iStockphoto/Getty Images, Grafissimo/iStockphoto/Getty Images, AleksandarPetrovic/iStockphoto/Getty Images; p. 42: jon chica parada/iStockphoto/Getty Images; p. 44: Wavebreakmedia/iStockphoto/Getty Images, joegolby/iStockphoto/Getty Images, londoneye/iStockphoto/Getty Images, Alex Raths/iStockphoto/Getty Images, Wavebreakmedia/iStockphoto/Getty Images, Ross Helen/iStockphoto/Getty Images; p. 50: kcline/iStockphoto/Getty Images, asiseeit/iStockphoto/Getty Images, rudisill/iStockphoto/Getty Images, Vladimir Vladimirov/iStockphoto/Getty Images; p. 54: flowgraph/iStockphoto/Getty Images, Alamy/Fotoarena, muratkoc/iStockphoto/Getty Images,

LuisPortugal/iStockphoto/Getty Images, syaber/iStockphoto/Getty Images, robynmac/iStockphoto/Getty Images, Mikhail Japaridze\TASS via Getty Images, Joan Pelissa, RoBeDeRo/iStockphoto/Getty Images, Dorling Kindersley/Getty Images,sergeichekman/iStockphoto/Getty Images, Michael Burrell/iStockphoto/Getty Images, PhotoEuphoria/iStockphoto/Getty Images, skodonnell/iStockphoto/Getty Images, nikkytok/iStockphoto/Getty Images, mariusz_prusaczyk/iStockphoto/Getty Images; p. 55: flowgraph/iStockphoto/Getty Images, artJazz/iStockphoto/Getty Images, Dino Geromella/iStockphoto/Getty Images, Petxeve/iStockphoto/Getty Images; p. 56: hadynyah/iStockphoto/Getty Images; p. 58: offstocker/iStockphoto/Getty Images, forest_strider/iStockphoto/Getty Images, Azure-Dragon/iStockphoto/Getty Images, davincidig/iStockphoto/Getty Images, ConstantinosZ/iStockphoto/Getty Images, ElementalImaging/iStockphoto/Getty Images; p. 64: Zurijeta/iStockphoto/Getty Images, karimhesham/iStockphoto/Getty Images, karimhesham/iStockphoto/Getty Images; p. 67: zemkooo/iStockphoto/Getty Images, Grafissimo/iStockphoto/Getty Images, VMJones/iStockphoto/Getty Images, Anolis01/iStockphoto/Getty Images; p. 72: dekihendrik/iStockphoto/Getty Images, Wjenningsphotography/iStockphoto/Getty Images, eyfoto/iStockphoto/Getty Images, AlexVey/iStockphoto/Getty Images, CreativeNature_nl/iStockphoto/Getty Images, CreativeNature_nl/iStockphoto/Getty Images; p. 74: Alamy/Fotoarena, Clement Peiffer/iStockphoto/Getty Images; p. 78: Poligrafistka/iStockphoto/Getty Images, sculpies/iStockphoto/Getty Images, oversnap/iStockphoto/Getty Images, Calin Stan/iStockphoto/Getty Images, Gladio1/iStockphoto/Getty Images, Byelikova_Oksana/iStockphoto/Getty Images, GeorgePeters/iStockphoto/Getty Images, JulNichols/iStockphoto/Getty Images, Marco Tulio/iStockphoto/Getty Images, AnthonyRosenberg/iStockphoto/Getty Images; p. 79: Viktorcvetkovic/iStockphoto/Getty Images, Squiddly/iStockphoto/Getty Images, Travel_Nerd/iStockphoto/Getty Images, zimmytws/iStockphoto/Getty Images; p. 80: szefei/iStockphoto/Getty Images; p. 82: VSanandhakrishna/iStockphoto/Getty Images; p. 88: Alamy/Fotoarena; p. 89: mitgirl/iStockphoto/Getty Images; p. 90: Alamy/Fotoarena, fotoVoyager/iStockphoto/Getty Images, JayKay57/iStockphoto/Getty Images; p. 92: Yobab/iStockphoto/Getty Images, izhairguns/iStockphoto/Getty Images, MediaProduction/iStockphoto/Getty Images, Dmytro Aksonov/iStockphoto/Getty Images, clubfoto/iStockphoto/Getty Images, venakr/iStockphoto/Getty Images; p. 98: VisitBritain/Martin Brent/Getty Images, LightFieldStudios/Martin Brent/Getty Images; p. 102: flowgraph/iStockphoto/Getty Images, katoosha/iStockphoto/Getty Images, SuhasiniDharmalingam/iStockphoto/Getty Images, Quanthem/iStockphoto/Getty Images, gerenme/iStockphoto/Getty Images, jaboticaba/iStockphoto/Getty Images, lila-es/iStockphoto/Getty Images, george tsartsianidis/iStockphoto/Getty Images, Photosbyjam/iStockphoto/Getty Images, tein79/iStockphoto/Getty Images, fotofermer/iStockphoto/Getty Images, twilightproductions/iStockphoto/Getty Images; p. 103: Leontura/iStockphoto/Getty Images, TheDman/iStockphoto/Getty Images, MoriaDemby/iStockphoto/Getty Images, coldsnowstorm/iStockphoto/Getty Images; p. 104: firina/iStockphoto/Getty Images; p. 106: MistikaS/iStockphoto/Getty Images, fotostok_pdv/iStockphoto/Getty Images, anilakkus/iStockphoto/Getty Images, julichka/iStockphoto/Getty Images, t_kimura/iStockphoto/Getty Images, Anthony DOUANNE/iStockphoto/Getty Images; p. 112: Fabio Colombini, mikehillpics/iStockphoto/Getty Images; p. 114: imagenavi/Getty Images; p. 116: Anthony Paz/iStockphoto/Getty Images, Bombaert/iStockphoto/Getty Images, W6/iStockphoto/Getty Images, dmitriymoroz/iStockphoto/Getty Images, onurdongel/iStockphoto/Getty Images, Firmafotografen/iStockphoto/Getty Images, CreativaStudio/iStockphoto/Getty Images; p. 122: NicolasMcComber/iStockphoto/Getty Images; p. 123: Ryan McVay/Getty Images; p. 126: VanReeel/iStockphoto/Getty Images, ©2018 Planet Labs, Inc., Jorge Araújo/Folhapress, Pascal Rondeau/Allsport/Getty Images, Agustin Vai/iStockphoto/Getty Images, xxmmxx/iStockphoto/Getty Images, Srdjan Stefanovic/iStockphoto/Getty Images, Justin Smith/iStockphoto/Getty Images, Geschaft/iStockphoto/Getty Images, Andrew_Rybalko/iStockphoto/Getty Images, pikepicture/iStockphoto/Getty Images; p. 127: Hermsdorf/iStockphoto/Getty Images, ©2018 Planet Labs, Inc., Age/Easypix, David Davies/PA Images/Getty Images.

Dados Internacionais de Catalogação na Publicação (CIP)
Bibliotecária responsável: Aline Graziele Benitez CRB-1/3129

C23n	Cant, Amanda
1.ed.	Next Station 1: Student's Book / Amanda Cant, Mary Charrington, Sarah Elizabeth Sprague; [Adapt.] Viv Lambert. – 1.ed. – São Paulo: Macmillan Education do Brasil, 2020.
	136 p.; il.; 21 x 27 cm. – (Coleção Next Station)
	ISBN: 978-85-511-0127-8
	1. Língua inglesa. I. Charrington, Mary. II. Sprague, Sarah Elizabeth. III. Lambert, Viv. IV. Título. V. Série.
	CDD 420

Índice para catálogo sistemático:
1. Língua inglesa

All rights reserved.

MACMILLAN EDUCATION DO BRASIL
Av. Brigadeiro Faria Lima, 1.309, 3º Andar –
Jd. Paulistano – São Paulo – SP – 01452-002
www.macmillan.com.br
Customer Service: [55] (11) 4613-2278
0800 16 88 77
Fax: [55] (11) 4612-6098

Printed in Brazil. Pancrom 10/2022

MAP STICKERS

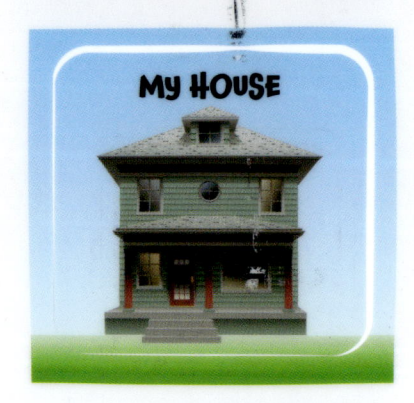

My House

·PASSPORT STICKERS·

- BRAZIL
- SHANGHAI CHINA — STATUS: ARRIVAL — SHANGHAI AIRPORT
- RUSSIA
- EGYPT
- UNITED KINGDOM
- USA
- JAPAN
- INDIA — Taj Mahal
- MEXICO
- WELCOME 15 JULY SPAIN — 40°26'N 3°42'W UTC+2